War, Global Capitalism and Resistance

Praise for *War, Global Capitalism and Resistance*

For the last twenty years, William I. Robinson has been developing a new theory of capitalism and the state; now his selected writings are collected in War, Global Capitalism and Resistance. His theory of capitalism, imperialism, and the state – describing a transnational capitalist world, a global police state, and the resistance to them – derives from earlier Marxists' theories but also transforms and develops them. His writings challenge us to rethink our understanding of capitalism and the class struggle. This compact book contributes to contemporary Marxist theory and should be widely read and debated on the left.

Dan La Botz, co-editor of *New Politics*, author of *The Nicaraguan Revolution: What Went Wrong? A Marxist Analysis*

William I. Robinson is without doubt one of the most outstanding and lucid writers on contemporary capitalism. Always thought-provoking and challenging, this compilation of his writings spanning almost three decades offers a compelling analysis of the changing nature of global capitalism today and how it has spawned mass migration, war, the rise of fascism, and the climate crisis. Essential reading for those seriously interested in better understanding the world around us.

Federico Fuentes, editor of LINKS,
International Journal of Socialist Renewal

William I. Robinson sheds light on the sociopolitical import of 21st century developments. He helps understand topics such as the phobic response to mass migration, the rise of the fascist far right, the many wars in the world, the genocide in Palestine and the climate crisis. His main insight is that global capitalism has taken over the whole world and operates as an integrated system controlled by a tiny transnational capitalist class bent on militarized accumulation at the expense of most of humanity and nature. Everyone who wants to stop capitalist globalization and build a better world must read this book.

Dr Trevor Ngwane, Director, Centre for Sociological
Research and Practice, University of Johannesburg

Resistance Books, London
resistancebooks.org | info@resistancebooks.org

Cover photograph: Anita Pouchard Serra

Cover and page design: NJ Catchpole

Typefaces: Cormorant (body), Aleo (headings)

paperback ISBN: 978-1-872242-21-7

e-pub ISBN: 978-1-872242-22-4

War, Global Capitalism and Resistance

Selected writings by William I. Robinson

Resistance Books, London

War, Global Capitalism and Resistance

Selected writings by William I. Robinson

Acknowledgments viii
Dedication ix
Author's preface xi
Introduction xiii

Globalization: Nine theses on our epoch 21
Global capitalism, migration labor, and the struggle for justice 42
Global capitalism and the restructuring of education 60
Capital has an International and it is going fascist 80
Passive revolution and the movement against mass incarceration . 89
Global capitalism post-pandemic 97
The travesty of "anti-imperialism" 109
Capitalist globalization, transnational class exploitation, and the global police state 123
Palestine and global crisis: Why genocide? Why now? 137

Notes and sources 150
Abbreviations 151
About the publishers 152

Acknowledgments

William I. Robinson has been developing an understanding of the changes to imperialism and global capitalism which deserve a wider distribution. Resistance Books greatly appreciates that William I. Robinson agreed to publish this collection of his writings with us.

Resistance Books is grateful to Kathy Lowe, Phil Hearse, and Dave Kellaway for their help and advice in the production of this book. Fred Leplat organized the production, and NJ Catchpole corrected the manuscript and designed the book. Without their contribution, it would not have been possible to publish *War, Global Capitalism and Resistance*.

The author and the publisher are thankful to the journals and publications who granted their permission to reprint the articles in this book.

Dedication

Dedicated to Neil Faulkner, who passed away unexpectedly in 2022. Those of us who knew him lost a dear friend and comrade. The global left lost a titan. Let his memory inspire us to continue forward in the struggle for socialism. The best tribute we can possibly make to the life of this exemplary revolutionary is to renew our commitment to the quest for a world free from exploitation and alienation.

William I. Robinson is Distinguished Professor of Sociology, Global Studies, and Latin American Studies at the University of California at Santa Barbara. Among his many award-winning books are *Can Global Capitalism Endure?* (Clarity Press, 2022); *Global Civil War: Capitalism Post-Pandemic* (Pm Press, 2022); *The Global Police State* (Pluto Press, 2020); *Into the Tempest: Essays on the New Global Capitalism* (Haymarket Books, 2018); *We Will Not Be Silenced: The Academic Repression of Israel's Critics* (Pluto Press, 2017, edited with Maryam Griffin); and *Global Capitalism and the Crisis of Humanity* (Cambridge University Press, 2014).

Author's preface
Humanity's existential crisis

We face overlapping threats to our very survival: the collapse of the planetary ecosystem, a third world war, and mass death as global capitalism undermines any possibility of social reproduction for billions of people. The ruling classes are turning to authoritarianism, dictatorship, and fascism to maintain their grip on power. Reformist elements among the elite may have alternative strategies for salvaging the system from the internal contradictions that are tearing it apart but in the long run they will not be able to resolve the existential crisis. That crisis is the outcome of the implacable drive to endlessly accumulate capital. Our only hope of survival is to struggle for a revolutionary ecosocialism from below that "expropriates the expropriators" and replaces the logic of private profit with that of social need and harmony with the rest of nature, and to do so before capitalism pushes us beyond the point of no return.

It is in the spirit of this fight for a socialist future that over the past three decades I have been writing articles and commentaries aimed at providing analyses of the turbulent times in which we live that are accessible to a public beyond the academy as my contribution to mass struggles against capitalism. I have strived in this endeavor to show how world capitalism entered a new transnational epoch in the late twentieth century that we must understand if our struggles are to be effective, for, as Sun Tzu put it in *The Art of War* – and we are certainly at war – "If you know the enemy and know yourself, your victory will not stand in doubt."

The comrades at Resistance Books chose a selection from among these essays to include in this book. The temptation was very great to update and even re-write any number of them since my thoughts have evolved over the past three decades. More importantly, world events have developed and global capitalism has continued to experience transformation so quickly that it is hard to keep up. Here and there I have inserted a few new sentences or paragraphs, cut back on details that are no longer important, or undertaken other sorts of updating. But by and large I chose a strategy of preserving the essays in their original form and placing them in chronological order of their original publication. One can trace in this way the evolution of my thinking and also observe how the overall framework of global capitalism theory remains vital to understanding the changing conditions under which our struggles press forward. I have also omitted here footnotes, endnotes and reference sections including in the original publications and direct readers to them for all sources. Thanks to Professor Oscar Soto who co-authored with me an earlier version of 'Passive Revolution and the Movement Against Mass Incarceration'.

I gratefully acknowledge permission granted by the journals *Race and Class, LINKS, Social Justice, Journal of World-Systems Research*, and *Race, Class, and Corporate Power* to reproduce here essays that were originally published in their pages.

William I. Robinson
Los Angeles, USA
February 2024

Introduction

Theory of crisis and crisis of theory

Phil Hearse, August 2024

Theory often lags behind reality. Many of today's radical activists cleave to a theoretical outlook they learned in the last quarter of the twentieth century. This view needs to be radically renewed to cope with today's reality.

The changes that have taken place over the last fifty years – such as the dramatic acceleration of global warming; the collapse of communism; the rise of China; the imposition of neoliberalism; globalization; and the rise of the semi-fascist far right – have rendered less relevant key aspects of Marxist theory that were developed in the 1970s and 80s. For example, the series of interviews with Ernest Mandel published in *New Left Review* in 1976–1978 (later published in the book *Revolutionary Marxism Today*[1]) pertain to a world that no longer exists and therefore has less power to explain today's capitalist order. That theorists fifty years ago did not foresee all the elements of the present crisis is because these elements were literally unforeseeable.

The revolutionary leaders of a hundred years ago – Lenin, Luxemburg, and Trotsky – did not simply repeat what Marx and Engels had said forty or fifty years earlier at the time of the Paris Commune. They developed the new theories needed to chart the global impact of the First World War and the wave of revolutions that followed it. These included, crucially, analysis of imperialism and its political consequences.

There have been many important works of Marxist theory since the turn of the millennium[2], but most of these have not attempted an overarching vision that integrates that series of interconnected phenomena that are nevertheless presented by the mass media as separate issues: mass migration, war, the rise of fascism, and the climate crisis.

Such an overarching view has now been developed by William I. Robinson, in *Global Capital and the Crisis of Humanity* (2014), *The*

Global Police State (2020), *Global Civil War* (2022), and *Can Capitalism Endure?* (2022), as well as in a series of online and magazine articles and academic papers that have elaborated and reinforced his theories. The most important of these pieces are now collected for the first time in this volume.

Central to Robinson's theoretical framework are the transnational capitalist class (TCC), the global police state, militarized accumulation, digital capitalism, and surplus humanity. Each of these concepts is underpinned by a conception of capitalist crisis as a recurring crisis of overproduction (of capital) and an underconsumption of commodities. Robinson's theory of crisis is compatible with key elements of the "orthodox" theories of crisis (for example, the Rosdolsky/Mandel school[3], and some of the key ideas of the *Monthly Review* school[4]).

Robinson adheres to the idea of long waves in capitalism, each lasting for about fifty years, but like Mandel he sees these waves being launched by exogenous events in society and politics, not as automatic events within the economy itself.

The idea of the TCC is that there is a decisive step towards the global integration of the giant monopolistic corporations, including those in banking, pharmaceuticals, computing and digital platforms, armaments, fossil fuels like oil and gas, mineral extraction, retailing, agribusiness, and "infotainment" (the vast interconnected world of movies, TV channels, news gathering, and music). These giants rest on top of the capitalist class as a whole and under the tutelage of finance capital centered in the United States.

Relations in the TCC are a complex web. The most popular Apple products like the iPhone and iPad are assembled in China, with components from Taiwan, South Korea, the United States, and Europe. The ownership of Apple includes major investors from China, the Gulf, and Europe. It is an internationalized corporation, although the majority of its shareholders are American.

The interests of states are not necessarily those of the TCC itself. States must balance the needs and local power of political formations and mass movements, and the bureaucracies of the national state itself, against the globalized interests of the TCC. That can be seen in China, where Xi Jinping and the Chinese Communist Party leadership have been engaged in a five-year process of bringing China-based banks to heel and forcing all major companies to assist with the work of the People's Liberation Army. In Russia, the conflict between the "oligarchs" and Vladimir Putin's base in the security apparatus is now an old story, but that does not mean the factions were clear-cut. Putin and his loyal supporters have emerged as new oligarchs, as well as securing the support of some old ones (like the former owner of Chelsea football club, Roman Abramovich).

Finance capital today includes some of the richest tech corporations such as Apple, Meta, Microsoft, Amazon, and Tesla. Their profits are so vast that they have accumulated cash mountains, often hidden in tax havens such as Ireland and Luxembourg, and are constantly seeking outlets for investment. These hoards of cash generally escape supervision and regulation by national states and international bodies like the EU. Modern finance capital requires the fastest possible turnover. This objective involves the creation of digital platforms like Amazon that capture huge amounts of data about customers.

State institutions, such as health and education, accumulate enormous quantities of data about individuals and organizations, too. Digital capitalism is also surveillance capitalism, with the United States and China at the forefront of developing these technologies. In effect, there are no barriers to security services and police forces using surveillance of computers and mobile phones to track political activity and real-time locations so that they can build a picture of dissident movements and individuals. Once this data is captured, there is no turning back. Short of major democratic upheavals, the information will remain in the system forever, especially as surveillance is shared internationally between security services and police forces.

We have now what Michel Foucault called a Panopticon state, after the prison designed by British philosopher Jeremy Bentham[5], which allowed the interior of each cell to be permanently viewed by prison guards. Of course, at any one time only a small number of prisoners *would* be viewed, but the fear of the possibility of being under surveillance modified the behavior of every prisoner. Similarly, we are nowadays aware that almost all of our speech and actions may be recorded by big tech and passed on to the police or security services – and this represses and undermines the possibilities of expressing dissident opinions.

Some of Robinson's book titles seem designed to annoy leftists schooled in the twentieth century. *Global Police State*? Surely police states are national, and some states are liberal democracies! *Global Civil War*? Surely civil wars are, by definition, national in scope, not international!

The idea of the global police state is shorthand for an integrated bundle of realities, which include the rise of fascism; the paramilitarization of police forces; sweeping new laws that make protestors liable to prosecution; the use of mass imprisonment and death squads against democratic and anti-system movements; and the increased use of police surveillance. These phenomena have risen sharply since the 2007–2008 financial crash and the imposition of harsh austerity, which forced the working class and other poor sections of the population to pay for another crisis of the system.

The global police state also includes the systems that exert control over asylum seekers and refugees, tens of thousands of whom have died trying to get into the United States and Europe on their perilous journeys through Panama and Guatemala to Mexico, and across the Mediterranean. These are truly the "surplus humanity" whose "illegal" status makes it possible for them to be drawn in and cast out at the whim of the states in which they seek refuge. The callous attitude of mainstream politicians to these waves of victimized humanity is a measure of the moral decay of the main pro-capitalist parties.

The "global police state" idea is connected to the concept of "militarized accumulation". The vast profits of corporations like Northrup-Grumman and Lockheed-Martin hide the overall weight of military production, because all the major tech companies provide massive services to the military. Amazon and Meta provide huge cloud-computing facilities to the U.S. military. Arms manufacture and export are central features of many British, Russian, and Chinese-based companies, and arms exports flood the markets of Africa, Asia, and Latin America, as well as European countries. Military imports include the huge supplies of anti-riot materials, at which Chinese-based companies excel.

Modern fascism is the term used in Robinson's writings to designate the "new fascist" phenomena of movements like Giorgia Meloni's Brothers of Italy, Marine Le Pen's Rassemblement National in France, and Vox in Spain. The interaction between street-fighting fascist gangs and hard-right demagogues like Donald Trump was on full display on January 6, 2021, at the storming of the U.S. Capitol Building in Washington. But for the most part, modern fascism tries to come to power through elections and transform the state from within. Robinson's notion of modern fascism closely aligns with the "creeping fascism" elaborated by the late Neil Faulkner and others.

In our discussions with Robinson in 2021–22, Faulkner and I drew attention to Guy Debord's theory of the "spectacle" of modern capitalism, the huge ideological array of images and events visible in advertising, movies, print media, social media, television, political rallies, etc., which today present capitalism as literally enthralling.[6] The spectacle, we argued, is vital to the turnover of commodities, from electronics to fashion and music events, which are available to the middle classes and to most permanently employed sections of the working class. Faulkner went further in trying to integrate Willhelm Reich's notion of the 'mass psychology of fascism' into this theoretical model.

Sustaining the consumerist spectacle requires building a mountain of debt racked up by corporations and individuals alike. This is the era of "fictitious" capital, in which the debt mountain of today prepares for the default and insolvency of the future. Indeed, the 2007–2008 financial crisis was never actually resolved; it was only temporarily overcome with the creation of more massive debt, also known as quantitative easing – truly fictitious capital.

It is now more difficult for the ruling class to maintain its grip on the mass media, as social media is less controllable. The fight to keep internet freedom is an important one for radicals and anti-capitalists.

Throughout Robinson's books, the theme emerges of a political polarization between left and right. The move towards police repression and fascism can only be explained by the emergence of dissident movements after the 2007–2008 financial crisis. These include the Arab Spring, the Hong Kong democracy movement, repeated general strikes in Greece, the Gilets Jaunes in France, and the Occupy and Black Lives Matter movements in the United States.

Less visible to radicals in Europe and North America have been the mass struggles in Asia and Latin America, from insurrection in Myanmar to the farmers' struggle in India and repeated, brutally repressed uprisings in Colombia. It is against these mass movements that the global civil war is being fought.

With democracy under threat nearly everywhere, and with the battle against the hard right now being fought over measures to curb global warming, a coherent socialist vision based on Marxist theory is urgently needed.

After Donald Trump was defeated in the November 2020 U.S. presidential election, some leftists took this to mean that the theory of creeping fascism had been disproved. Then, just two months later, on January 6, 2021, Joe Biden's inauguration was disrupted by the previously mentioned attempted insurrection by Trump supporters at the U.S. Capitol building. Regrettably, since then it has become obvious in Italy, France, Germany, Spain, Portugal, and the United States itself that the fascist and far-right demagogues and their parties have not gone away.

As these words are being penned, brutal wars are being fought in Ukraine and Palestine. Less visible to TV audiences is the war in Sudan, where civilians have been subjected to every kind of brutality; it is highly unlikely that the death toll there is less than in Palestine. In the Democratic Republic of Congo (DRC), an ongoing genocide is restarting against villagers and communities, with Uganda and Rwanda both backing powerful local militias in the fight to control the production of minerals used in high-tech devices, as well as diamonds and gold. The people in both Sudan and the DRC are experiencing fearful sexual violence on an unprecedented scale.

Militarized accumulation is on full display in these conflicts, with weapons from the USA, Russia, Britain, and China in use; we are living in a boom time for manufacturers of every type of weapon.

Against these dangerous tendencies, the trade union movement has been experiencing a revival in Britain and the United States in particular. Hundreds of thousands of workers were involved in the UK health and transport strikes in 2023 alone.

The movement against the war on Palestine and in solidarity with the Palestinian people has become truly global. Hundreds of thousands of people mobilized on the streets of Britain on successive weekends; as Robinson points out, this has been paralleled in the United States and in many other countries.

Robinson identifies himself as an ecosocialist, although he is not a theorist of climate change as such. Rather, his work on the immigration crisis and "surplus humanity" sees global heating and its likely consequences as causing devastation on the borders of the capitalist core states. Commenting on an article by Gaia Vince[7], which claims that advanced capitalist states and cities will be competing for immigrants by the mid-twenty-first century because of demographic decline, Robinson has expressed the view[8] that it is much more likely that the political leaders of the global North's richest states would rather tolerate mass death events on their borders than admit large numbers of refugees. This is not because of a rational calculation of economic self-interest, but because anti-immigrant nationalism is now at the core of the political self-interest of the mainstream parties and the hard right alike.

For sure, we live in a world of immense danger and immense opportunities. Humanity must be dragged towards facing up to the consequences of climate change, economic crisis, and creeping fascism.

The speed with which vaccines were developed to fight the Covid-19 pandemic and the upcoming potential of artificial intelligence speak to the huge possibilities for humanity if we can create a society based on democracy and egalitarianism. Otherwise, we face deepening mass poverty, war, and climate collapse. The disastrous consequences of the war in Gaza, where tens of thousands of people have been killed, is perhaps the first mass death event at the borders of the Global North. War and economic collapse are creating other mass death events in Sudan, Tigre, and Ukraine. The latter has so far seen a death toll that may have reached two hundred thousand, counting both Russian and Ukrainian troops.

We are certainly living in a world where militarized accumulation is gaining yet more ground, as more billions of dollars in sales and aid are poured into competing armies. This includes the vast arms sales and donations to Israel and Ukraine, but also huge sales by China to the Myanmar generals, and by Russia to reactionary states like Uganda.

The work of William I. Robinson shines a light on the reality of the world today, and on the tasks that the radical left must face.

Notes on the introduction

[1] (1979), Verso.

[2] See, for example: Cedric Durand, Fictitious Capital (2017), Verso; David Harvey, Rebel Cities (2010), Verso; Gilbert Achcar, The People Want (2012), Al-Saqi Books; Morbid Symptoms (2016), Al-Saqi Books; The New Cold War (2023), Westbourne Press; Michael Löwy, Ecosocialism (2015), Haymarket Books; Peter Gowan, The Global Gamble (2009), Verso; Mike Davis, Planet of Slums (2006), Verso; The Monster Enters (2022), Verso.

[3] See Ernest Mandel, Late Capitalism (1975), Verso; Long Waves of Capitalist Development (1980); Verso, https://files.libcom.org/files/ernest-mandel-long-waves-of-capitalist-development-a-marxist-interpretation.pdf; Roman Rosdolsky, The Making of Marx's Capital volumes 1 and 2 (1992), Pluto Press; Ernest Mandel, Late Capitalism (1975), Verso.

[4] See Paul Baran and Paul Sweezy, Monopoly Capital (1966), Monthly Review Press.

[5] https://en.wikipedia.org/wiki/Panopticon.

[6] Guy Debord, Society of the Spectacle (1967), Marxist Internet Archive, https://www.marxists.org/reference/archive/debord/society.htm; Douglas Kellner and Stephen Best, Debord and the Postmodern Turn, https://pages.gseis.ucla.eduaculty/kellner/essays/debordpostmodernturn.pdf; Michael Löwy, Consumed by Night's Fire (1998), Radical Philosophy, https://www.radicalphilosophy.com/article/consumed-by-nights-fire; Phil Hearse, Guy Debord and the Spectacle (2021), Anti-Capitalist Resistance, https://anticapitalistresistance.org/guy-debord-and-the-spectacle/.

[7] Gaia Vince, The century of climate migration: why we need to plan for the great upheaval (2022), The Guardian, https:// www.theguardian.com/news/2022/aug/18/century-climate-crisis-migration-why-we-need-plan-great-upheaval.

[8] Email exchange between author and Robinson.

Globalization: Nine theses on our epoch

First published in *Race and Class*, 1996

The left and progressives around the world have been struggling for several decades now to come to terms with the fundamental dynamic of our epoch: capitalist globalization. The globalization of capitalism, and the transnationalization of social, political, and cultural processes it entails, is the world-historic context of developments as the twenty-first century progresses. The debate on globalization continues to play out in the academy, and, more importantly, among diverse social and political movements worldwide. These movements have run up against globalizing processes that are redefining the very terrain of social action, including the deep constraints, as well as real opportunities, that the new global environment presents for popular change. In my view, however, activists and scholars alike have tended to understate the *systemic* nature of the changes involved in globalization, which is redefining the fundamental reference points of human society and social analysis, and requires a modification of existing paradigms.

Capitalist globalization denotes a world war. This war was brewing for four decades following WWII, concealed behind a whole set of secondary contradictions tied up with the Cold War and the East–West conflict. It was incubated with the development of new technologies and the changing face of production and of labor in the capitalist world and with the incubation of transnational capital out of former national capitals in the North. The opening salvos date back to the early 1980s, when, as I argue below, class fractions representing transnational capital gained effective control of state apparatuses in the North and set about to capture these apparatuses in the South. This war has proceeded with the liberation of transnational capital from any constraint to its global activity that came with the demise of the former Soviet bloc and with the increasing achievement by capital of total mobility and of access to every corner of the world. It is a war of a global rich and powerful minority against the global poor, dispossessed, and outcast majority.

Casualties already number in the hundreds of millions, and threaten to mount into the billions. I refer to this as a world war *figuratively*, in that the level of social conflict and human destruction has reached bellicose proportions. But I also mean so *literally*, in that the conflict bound up with capitalist globalization is truly a *world* war: it involves all peoples around the world, and none can escape involvement.

Describing the current state of affairs as a *world war* is a dramatic statement, intended to underscore the extent to which I believe humanity has entered a period that could well rival or even surpass the colonial depredations of past centuries. However, I do not mean to be apocalyptic or dispiriting. As I discuss below, capitalist globalization is a *process*, not so much consummated as in motion. It confronts major contradictions that present the possibilities of altering its course. A more precise reading of capitalist globalization is therefore required as a guide to our social inquiry and our action. What follows, far from a claim to resolve the debate on globalization, is a modest attempt to take stock of the principal contours of our epoch. It is intended to present a holistic snapshot of the globalization "forest" by identifying its most imperious trees and their interconnections, in accord with what I believe should be key theoretical and practical concerns of intellectuals and activists.

First, the essence of the process is the replacement, for the first time in the history of the modern world capitalist system, of all residual pre (or non)-capitalist production relations with capitalist ones in every part of the globe.

Activists and scholars have noted that globalization involves the hastened internationalization of capital and technology; a new international division of labor; economic integration processes; a decline in the importance of the nation-state; and so on. The world has been moving in the past few decades toward a situation in which nations have been linked, via capital flows and exchange in an integrated international market, to the globalization of the process of production itself. In turn, economic globalization is bringing with it the material basis for the transnationalization of political processes and systems, of civil societies, and the global integration of social life. Globalization has increasingly eroded national boundaries and made it structurally impossible for individual nations to sustain independent, or even autonomous, economies, polities, and social structures. Nation-states are no longer appropriate units of analysis.

These are all important features. But the core of globalization, theoretically conceived, is the near culmination of a process that began with the dawn of European colonial expansion and the modern world system over 500 years ago: the gradual spread of capitalist production around the world and its displacement of all pre-capitalist relations. (Of course, it is impossible for all social relations to be capitalist; human society would collapse if every single interaction were based on exchange value. More technically, what is taking place is *the formal subsumption of all peoples to capital, and, as well, the accelerated shift from formal to real subsumption.*) From a world in which capitalism was the dominant mode within a system of "articulated modes of production," globalization is bringing about a world integrated into a single capitalist mode (thus, *capitalist* globalization). This involves all the changes associated with capitalism, but changes that are *transnational* rather than national or *inter*national in character. It includes the transnationalization of classes and the accelerated division of all of humanity into just two classes – global capital and global labor – although both remain embedded in segmented structures and hierarchies.

Global capitalism is tearing down all non-market structures that have in the past placed limits on the accumulation – and the dictatorship – of capital. Every corner of the globe, every nook and cranny of social life is becoming commodified. This involves breaking up and commodifying non-market spheres of human activity, namely public spheres managed by states and private spheres linked to community and family units and to local and household economies. This complete commodification of social life is undermining what remains of democratic control by people over the conditions of their daily existence, above and beyond that which is involved with private ownership of the principal means of production. As James O'Connor has noted, we are seeing the maturation of the capitalist *economy* into capitalist *society*, with the penetration of capitalist relations into all spheres of life.

Commodification involves the transfer to capital of both formerly public spheres and formerly non-capitalist private spheres such as family and cultural realms. All around the world, the public sphere, including educational and health systems, police forces, prisons, utilities, infrastructure, and transportation systems, is being privatized and commodified. The juggernaut of exchange value is also invading intimate private spheres of community, family, and culture. None of the old pre-commodity spheres provide a protective shield from the alienation of capitalism. In every aspect of our social existence, we increasingly interact with our fellow human beings through dehumanized and competitive commodity relationships.

Second, a new "social structure of accumulation" is emerging which, for the first time in history, is global.

A social structure of accumulation refers to a set of mutually reinforcing social, economic, and political institutions and cultural and ideological norms that fuse with and facilitate a successful pattern of capital accumulation over specific historic periods. A new global social structure of accumulation is becoming superimposed on, and transforming, existing national social structures of accumulation. Integration into the global system is the causal structural dynamic that underlies the events we have witnessed in nations and regions all around the world over the past few decades. The breakup of national economic, political, and social structures is reciprocal to the gradual breakup, starting in the latter decades of the twentieth century, of a pre-globalization nation-state-based world order. New economic, political, and social structures emerge as each nation and region becomes integrated into emergent transnational structures and processes.

The agent of the global economy is transnational capital, organized institutionally in global corporations and in supranational economic planning agencies and political forums, such as the International Monetary Fund (IMF), the Trilateral Commission, the G7 forum, and the World Economic Forum, and managed by a class-conscious transnational elite based in the centers of world capitalism but increasingly present outside of these centers. This transnational elite has an integrated global agenda of mutually reinforcing economic, political, and cultural components that, taken together, comprise a new global social structure of accumulation.

The economic component is *hyper-liberalism*, which seeks to achieve the conditions for the total mobility and unfettered worldwide activity of capital. Hyper-liberalism includes the elimination of state intervention in the economy and regulation by individual nation-states of the activity of transnational capital in their territories. It is putting an end to the state's earlier ability to interfere with profit-making by capturing and redistributing surpluses. In the North, hyper-liberalism, first launched by the Reagan and Thatcher governments, takes the form of deregulation and the dismantling of Keynesian welfare states. In the South, it involves "neoliberal structural adjustment" programs. These programs seek macroeconomic stability (price and exchange rate stability, etc.) as an essential requisite for the activity of transnational capital, which must harmonize a wide range of fiscal, monetary, and industrial policies among multiple nations if it is to be able to function simultaneously, and often instantaneously, among numerous national borders.

The political component, at least up until the first decade of the twenty-first century, has been the development of political systems that operate through consensual rather than through direct, coercive domination. As globalization unfolded, consensual mechanisms of social control tended to replace dictatorships, authoritarianism, and repressive colonial systems that characterized much of the world's formal political authority structures right up to the post-Cold War period. The transnational elite refers to these political systems as "democracy," although there is little or no authentic democratic content. The "democratic consensus" in the new world order is a consensus among an increasingly cohesive global elite on the type of political system most propitious to the reproduction of social order in the new global environment. Escalating political instability and social conflict around the world make it increasingly difficult to maintain "democratic" systems. Indeed, as global crisis deepens, we are already seeing a reversion to dictatorships and openly authoritarian systems, and even to fascism.

The cultural/ideological component is consumerism and cutthroat individualism. Consumerism proclaims that wellbeing, peace of mind, and purpose in life are achieved through the acquisition of commodities. Competitive individualism legitimizes personal survival, and whatever is required to achieve it, over collective wellbeing. Consumerism and individualism imbue mass consciousness at the global level. They channel mass aspirations into individual consumer desires, even though these induced wants will never be met for the vast majority of humanity. The culture and ideology of global capitalism thus works to depoliticize social behavior and preempt collective action aimed at social change by channeling people's activities into a fixation on the search for individual consumption and survival.

Globalization, therefore, has profound consequences for each nation of the world system. Productive structures in each nation are reorganized reciprocally to a new international division of labor, characterized by the concentration of finances, services, technology, and knowledge in the North, and the labor-intensive phases of globalized production in the South. However, this new international division of labor has been giving way to a global division of labor as the great North–South divide (what used to be called the First World–Third World divide) begins to erode. As each national economy is restructured and subordinated to the global economy, new activities linked to globalization come to dominate. Pre-globalization classes such as national peasantries, small-scale artisans, and domestic bourgeoisies linked to national capital and internal markets, are weakened and threatened with disintegration. New groups linked to the global economy emerge and become dominant, both economically and politically. States are externalized. Political systems are shaken and reorganized. The dominant global culture penetrates, perverts, and reshapes cultural institutions, group identities, and mass consciousness.

Third, this transnational agenda has germinated in every country of the world under the guidance of hegemonic transnationalized fractions of national bourgeoisies.

Global capitalism is represented in each nation-state by in-country representatives, who constitute transnationalized fractions of dominant groups. The *international class alliance* of national bourgeoisies into the post-WWII period has mutated into a *transnationalized bourgeoisie* in the post-Cold War period, by the 1990s it had become the hegemonic class fraction globally. This denationalized bourgeoisie is class-conscious, and conscious of its transnationality. At its apex is a managerial elite that controls the levers of global policymaking, and which responds to transnational finance capital as the hegemonic fraction of capital on a world scale.

In the 1970s and 1980s, incipient transnationalized fractions set out to eclipse national fractions in the core capitalist countries of the North and to capture the "commanding heights" of state policymaking. From the 1980s into the 1990s, these fractions became ascendant in the South and began to vie for, and in many countries, capture state apparatuses. By the *fin de siècle*, the transnational agenda was embryonic in some countries and regions (e.g., much of sub-Sahara Africa). It had incubated and was ascendant in other regions (e.g., major portions of Asia). It became fully consolidated elsewhere (e.g., in much of Latin America). Given the structures of North–South asymmetry, transnationalized fractions in the Third World are "junior" partners. In the late twentieth and early twenty-first centuries, under the tutelage of their "senior" counterparts in the North, they oversaw, at the local level, sweeping economic, political, social, and cultural changes involved in globalization, including free-market reform, the fomenting of "democratic" systems in place of dictatorships, and the dissemination of the culture/ideology of consumerism and individualism.

Fourth, observers search for a new global "hegemon" and posit a tri-polar world of European, American, and Asian economic blocs. But the old nation-state phase of capitalism has been superseded by the transnational phase of capitalism.

In his master study, *The Great Transformation*, Karl Polanyi summed up the previous historic change in the relationship between the state and capital, and society and market forces, that took place with the maturation of national capitalism in the nineteenth century and the first half of the twentieth. Since the late twentieth century we have been witness to another unfolding "great transformation," the maturation of *transnational capitalism*.

But activists and scholars still cling on to an outdated nation-state framework of analysis that reifies the state, with a consequent misreading of events and the danger of misdirected social action. The momentary fluxes, conflicts, and contradictions bound up with the transition from national to transnational capitalism should not be confused with the historic tendency itself. Globalization changes the relationship between capitalism and territoriality, and with it the relationship between classes and the nation-state. The structural power of mobile transnational capital has been increasingly superimposed over the direct power of nation-states as the "commanding heights" of state decision-making shift toward webs of supranational institutions. The historic relation between nation-states and formerly nation-based classes, and between class power and state power, has been modified and requires redefinition.

The transnational bourgeoisie exercises its class power through two channels. One is a dense network of supranational institutions and relationships that increasingly bypass formal states, and that should be conceived of as an emergent transnational state that has not acquired any centralized institutional form. The other is the utilization of national governments, as territorially bound juridical units (the inter-state system) are transformed into transmission belts and filtering devices for the imposition of the transnational agenda. At the same time, transnational capitalists and elites in each country have captured their respective national states, or at least key ministries in these states, from where they promote the transnational agenda, so that national states become *proactive agents* of globalization. Transnational capital requires that nation-states perform three functions: 1) adopt fiscal and monetary policies which assure macroeconomic stability; 2) provide the basic infrastructure necessary for global economic activity (highways, telecommunications systems, educational systems for training global workers, etc.); and 3) provide social control, order, and stability. (The transnational elite assessed in the late 20th century that "democracy" is better able than dictatorship to perform this social-order function, as discussed below, but this may be changing as global crisis deepens.) In a nutshell, we are not witnessing "the death of the nation-state," but its transformation into *neoliberal states*.

It is true, therefore, as many scholars and activists have pointed out, that capital still needs state power. However, state power and the nation-state are not co-equivalent, and the interests of transnational capital do not correspond to any "national" interest or any nation-state. The confusion is in equating capital's need for the services provided by neoliberal states, and the use it makes of the lingering inter-state system, with some type of organic affinity between transnational capital and specific nation-states, as existed in the national stage of capitalism. If major concentrations of transnational capital are no longer associated with any particular nation-state, on what material and class basis should inter-state conflict be interpreted? What theoretical rationale exists for predicting rivalry and competition between nation-states as an expression of the competition of national capitals?

The spatial decentralization of the power of transnational capital has been confused with a growing "strength" and "independence" of "U.S. rivals," and with geopolitical shifts in power conceived in terms of nation-states. In fact, transnational capital and its principal institutional agent, the global corporation, are able to exploit an antiquated nation-state/inter-state system to wring further concessions from global labor. The continued separation of the world into nation-states creates a central condition for the power of transnational capital.

An outdated nation-state framework can misread events. Although it was the Reagan government of the 1980s that first launched globalization in the United States, at the time many commentators interpreted Reaganism as a retrograde right-wing project opposed to a more "liberal" program. Since then, all U.S. administrations and the core of both the Democratic and Republican parties have pushed capitalist globalization. The differences among these administrations have not represented a fundamental clash between distinct capitalist fractions or projects, but differences over the pace, timing, and secondary aspects (e.g., social policy) of advancing the transnational agenda in the United States. The fundamental restructuring of social policies that began under Reaganism and Thatcherism in the North were not the product of conservative movements and right-wing political inclinations, per se, despite appearance. Rather, they represented the logical concrete policy and ideological adjuncts of globalization as it applied to the particular conditions of each country.

Similarly, tactical differences between national governments of core countries over how to advance transnational interests – tactical differences often originating in the particulars of local and regional histories and conditions – take on the appearance of fundamental contradictions between rival "national capitals" and "national interests." Events may *appear* as contradictions between nation-states when in *essence* they are often contradictions internal to global capitalism. The need for neoliberal states to secure legitimacy as part of their social-order function often entails a discourse of "national interests," "foreign competition," and so on, at the ideological and the mass public levels. Suffice it to recall that the hallmark of good social analysis is to distinguish appearance from essence.

For instance, the Trump government that came to power in 2017 put forth a nationalist and populist discourse, yet the actual content of its policies represented an intensification of neoliberalism in the face of an increasingly severe global crisis. In fact, the election of Trump reflected precisely a far-right response, tinged by twenty-first century fascist currents, to the crisis of global capitalism. As with other "right-wing populist" and far-right movements in recent years, Trumpism was a response to the crises of state legitimacy in the face of the extreme polarization of wealth unleashed by globalization, and the increasing insecurity, downward mobility, and even immiseration, of major sectors of the U.S. working class. The crisis of state legitimacy has resulted in an increase in *inter*-national or geopolitical tensions – however, these have to be understood in a different light from earlier national rivalries based on competing national capitalist classes.

Fifth, the "brave new world" of global capitalism is profoundly anti-democratic.

Global capitalism is predatory and parasitic. In today's global economy, capitalism is less benign, less responsive to the interests of broad majorities around the world, and less accountable to society than ever before. At the end of the twentieth century, some 400 transnational corporations had come to own two-thirds the planet's fixed assets and control 70 per cent of world trade. With the world's resources controlled by a few hundred global corporations, the lifeblood and the very fate of humanity is in the hands of transnational capital, which holds the power to make life-and-death decision for millions of human beings. Such tremendous concentrations of economic power lead to tremendous concentrations of political power at the global level. Any discussion of "democracy" under such conditions becomes meaningless.

The paradox of the demise of dictatorships, "democratic transitions," and the spread of "democracy" around the world that took place in the late twentieth and early twenty-first centuries was to be explained by new forms of social control, and the misuse of the concept of democracy, the original meaning of which, the power (*cratos*) of the people (*demos*), has been reconfigured beyond recognition. What the transnational elite calls democracy is more accurately termed *polyarchy*, to borrow a concept from academia. Polyarchy is neither dictatorship nor democracy, at the level of the political system. It refers to a system in which a small group rules, on behalf of capital, and participation in decision-making by the majority is confined to choosing among competing elites in tightly controlled electoral processes. This "low-intensity democracy" is a form of *consensual domination*. Social control and domination are *hegemonic*, in the sense meant by the great Italian socialist thinker Antonio Gramsci, rather that coercive. It is based less on outright repression than on diverse forms of ideological co-optation and political disempowerment made possible by the structural domination and "veto power" of global capital.

Starting in the 1980s and coinciding with the onslaught of capitalist globalization, the transnational elite began to promote polyarchy in the global South and around the world ("democracy promotion"), in tandem with neoliberalism. This was in contrast to the earlier global network of civilian-military regimes and outright dictatorships (e.g., the Somozas, the Duvaliers, the Marcos, the Pinochets, and white minority regimes), and, before them, repressive colonial states, that the Northern capitalist countries had promoted and sustained for much of modern world history. Authoritarian systems tended to unravel as globalizing pressures broke up embedded forms of coercive political authority, dislocated traditional communities and social patterns, and stirred masses of people to demand the democratization of social life. Disorganized masses pushed for a deeper popular democratization, while organized elites pushed for tightly controlled transitions from authoritarianism and dictatorships to elite polyarchies.

This issue is crucial, because in the twentieth century, much of the left worldwide was not democratic, either within its own organizations or in state practices in those countries where it came to power. The left's historic democratic failings have made some hesitant to denounce polyarchy for what it is: a mockery of democracy. The left must be committed to democracy in society and in its own institutions – a popular, participatory democracy from the grassroots up that empowers popular classes at the local level, that subordinates states to civil society, that holds leaders accountable, and so on. But the Stalinist political system in the former Soviet bloc had little to do with democracy, and nor does contemporary polyarchy.

The trappings of democratic procedure in a polyarchy do not mean that the lives of the mass of people become filled with authentic or meaningful popular democratic content, much less that social justice or greater economic equality is achieved. The new polyarchies ("the new democracies" in the lexicon of the transnational elite) of emergent global society did not, *and were not intended to*, meet the authentic aspirations of repressed and marginalized majorities for political participation, for greater socioeconomic justice, or for cultural realization. As the twenty-first century progresses, the contradictions of global capitalism become ever more explosive. It is not clear whether the fragile polyarchies that still characterize the political systems of most countries around the world can absorb mounting crises of social control and legitimacy. There may be a return to dictatorial and authoritarian forms of control, and the rise of twenty-first century forms of fascism.

Sixth, "poverty amidst plenty": under globalization, socioeconomic inequalities and human misery are experiencing dramatic growth in nearly every country and region of the world, a consequence of the unbridled operation of transnational capital.

The dual tendency is that the gap between rich and poor is widening *within* each country, North and South alike, simultaneous to a sharp increase of the inequalities *between* the North and the South. Wealth is increasingly concentrated within a privileged strata encompassing some 20 per cent of humanity. The worldwide inequality in the distribution of wealth and power is a form of permanent structural violence against the world's majority. This is a widely noted phenomenon, but it needs to be linked more explicitly to globalization.

In 1992, the United Nations Development Program (UNDP) began publishing its annual *Human Development Report*, which chronicles levels of social development (or underdevelopment), poverty, and inequality worldwide. The report that year indicated that the wealthiest 20 per cent of humanity received 82.7 per cent of the world's wealth. Fast-forward to 2015: according to a report released that year by the international development agency Oxfam, the richest 20 per cent of humanity owned 94.5 per cent of the world's wealth while the remaining 80 per cent had to make do with just 5.5 per cent of that wealth.

According to a 2010 UNDP report, 1.5 billion people worldwide lived in extreme poverty that year, which was defined as making less than $1.25 dollars a day. Another 900 million were at risk of slipping into extreme poverty. In other words, some 35 per cent of humanity lived on the threshold between life and death. In all, 3 billion people earned less than $2.50 a day, a billion were without access to health services, 1.3 billion had no access to safe water, and 1.9 billion lacked access to adequate sanitation.

Global poverty and inequality are often measured as the gap between rich and poor countries, or North and South. There is indeed an abyss between the rich and poor nations when measured in in terms of nation-states, and it continues to widen. In 1960, the wealthiest twenty of the world's nations were thirty times richer than the poorest 20 per cent. Thirty years later, in 1990, they were sixty times richer, according to the 1994 UNDP report. The report noted, however, that "these figures conceal the true scale of injustice since they are based on comparisons of the average per capita incomes of rich and poor *countries*. In reality, of course, there are wide disparities within each country between rich and poor *people*" (emphasis in original). Adding the maldistribution within countries, the richest 20 per cent of the world's *people* got at least 150 times more than the poorest 20 per cent. In other words, the ratio of inequality between the global rich and the global poor (seen as social groups in a highly stratified world system) was 1:150.

The classical and more contemporary theories of imperialism, world-systems theory, and international political economy theories emphasize the outward drainage of surplus from the South to the North. The 1994 UNDP report noted that in 1992 the outflow in debt service charges alone (a figure which therefore does not include profit repatriation and other forms of surplus transfer from South to North) on the Third World's combined debt of $1.5 trillion was 2.5 times the total of Northern development aid, and $60 billion more than total private flows to developing countries. These "open veins" through which wealth continues to flow from South to North suggest that transnational capital operates in such a way that it still requires strategic rearguards in the core of world capitalism, where global management, the store of capital, and the centers of technology and finances are concentrated within a changing global division of labor.

But the perpetuation of the North–South or center–periphery divide does not translate into continued prosperity for majorities in the North. Simultaneous with the widening of the North–South divide, there has been a widening gap between rich and poor in the developed countries, along with heightened social polarization and political tensions. Between 1973 and 2015, real wages stagnated for 80 per cent of the U.S. population and rose for the remaining 20 per cent. In 2015, some 50 million people in the United States lived in poverty, and tens of millions more lived near the poverty level. The top quintile in the United States increased its share of income from 41.1 per cent in 1973 to 51 per cent in 2015, while the lowest quintile earned only 3.1 per cent of national income, and the richest one per cent had more income than the bottom 90 per cent. The concentration of wealth (which includes income and assets) was even more pronounced. Already in 1991, the top .05 per cent of the population owned 45.4 per cent of all assets, excluding homes. The top 1 per cent owned 53.2 per cent of all assets, and the top 10 per cent owned 83.2 per cent. The United States *belonged* to a tiny minority. The pattern is similar in other developed countries of the Organization of Economic Cooperation and Development (OECD).

The Occupy Wall Street movement of 2011–12 brought to worldwide attention the concentration of the world's wealth in the hands of 'the one percent' with its famous rallying cry, "We are the 99 percent!" Indeed, according to the Oxfam report mentioned above, the top 1 per cent of humanity owned an incredible 50 per cent of the planet's wealth in 2015. An even more significant contrast is between that better-off 20 per cent of humanity whose basic material needs are met, that has access the fruits of the global cornucopia and that generally enjoys conditions of security and stability, and the remaining 80 per cent of the world's people who face escalating poverty, deprivation, insecurity, and precariousness.

The North–South divide is growing and should not be understated. However, humanity is increasingly stratified along transnational class lines. Lakes of wealth in Third World countries and seas of poverty in First World countries are increasingly being created under globalization. New centers of global management, technology, and finance are rising in places such as China and India. Given these developments, it makes more sense to see the world as increasingly divided along class lines than along national lines. There are important empirical processes such as downward "global leveling" and theoretical issues that these processes raise which I will take up in later chapters.

Seventh, there are deep and interwoven racial, ethnic, and gender dimensions to this escalating global poverty and inequality.

As global capital concentrates, it disproportionately locks out racially and ethnically oppressed groups, and women. As transnational capital moves to the South of the world, it does not leave behind in the North, or encounter in the South, homogenous working classes, but ones which are historically stratified and segmented along racial, ethnic, and gender lines. In the North, for instance, labor of color was originally drawn, often by force, from the periphery to the core as menial labor. These workers are now disproportionately excluded from strategic economic sectors, instead being relegated to the ranks of the growing army of "supernumeraries." They labor in the most vulnerable sectors in a racially-segmented labor market which is becoming *more* rigid under globalization, and are subject to a rising tide of racism, including the dismantling of affirmative action programs and repressive state measures against immigrant labor pools.

Although globalizing processes are undermining the existence of pre-capitalist classes, they are also intensifying stratification among labor, often along racial/ethnic lines, in both North and South. However, I suggest that such hierarchies of labor are becoming spatially organized *across* the North–South axis, given global integration processes, new migration patterns, and increased concentrations of Third World labor in the First World, as well as the increasing impoverishment of once-privileged "labor aristocracies" of European origin.

The roots of the subordination of women – unequal participation in a sexual division of labor on the basis of the female reproductive function – are exacerbated by globalization, which increasingly turns women from reproducers of the labor power required by capital into reproducers of supernumeraries for which capital has no use. Women's labor is further devalued, and women denigrated, as the function of the domestic (household) economy moves from rearing labor for *incorporation* into capitalist production to rearing supernumeraries. This is one important structural underpinning of the global "feminization of poverty" and is reciprocal to, and mutually reinforces, racial/ethnic dimensions of inequality. It helps explain the movement among Northern elites to dismantle Keynesian welfare benefits in a manner which disproportionately affects women and racially oppressed groups, the relentless attacks on reproductive rights, and the impetuousness with which the neoliberal model calls for the elimination of even minimal social spending and safety nets that often mean, literally, the difference between life and death.

Eight, there are deep contradictions in emergent world society that make entirely uncertain the very survival of our species, much more the mid- to long-term stabilization and viability of global capitalism, and portend prolonged global social conflict.

The structure of global production, distribution, and consumption increasingly reflects the skewed income pattern. For instance, under the new global social apartheid, tourism is the fastest-growing economic activity, and even the mainstay of many Third World economies. This does not mean that more people are actually enjoying the fruits of leisure and international travel; it means that 20 per cent of humanity has more and more disposable income, while the consumption by the remaining 80 per cent contracts. This 80 per cent is forced to provide all sorts of ever more frivolous services, and to orient its productive activity toward meeting the needs and satisfying the sumptuous desires of that 20 per cent. By the turn of century, private security forces and prisons had become the number-one growth sector in the United States and the other Northern countries. Social apartheid spawns decadence. Militarized fortress cities and spatial apartheid are necessary for social control under circumstances in which an ever-smaller portion of humanity can afford to consume the essentials of life, let alone luxury goods.

As national capitalism in the North matured in the late nineteenth century, the tendency inherent in capital accumulation toward a concentration of income and productive resources, and the social polarity and political conflict this generates, was offset by two factors. The first was the intervention of states to regulate the operation of the free market, to guide accumulation, and to capture and redistribute surpluses. The second was the emergence of modern imperialism to offset the polarizing tendencies inherent in the process of capital accumulation in the North, such that global social conflict was generally transferred to the South. Both these factors therefore *fettered*, in the core of the world system, the social polarity generated by capitalism. But by reducing or eliminating the ability of individual states to regulate capital accumulation and capture surpluses, globalization is now bringing about precisely the polarization between a rich minority and a poor majority that Karl Marx predicted. Yet this time there are no "new frontiers," no virgin lands for capitalist colonization that could offset the social and political consequences of global polarization.

Endemic to unfettered global capitalism, therefore, is intensified social conflict, which in turn engenders constant political crises and ongoing instability, both within countries and between them. In the post-WWII period, the North was able to shift much social conflict to the South as a combined result of an imperialist transfer of wealth from South to North and the redistribution of this wealth in the North through Keynesian state intervention. No less than 160 wars were fought in the Third World from 1945 to 1990. However, globalization involves a distinct shift in global strife from inter-state conflict (reflecting a certain correspondence between classes and nations in the stage of national capitalism) to global class conflict. The UNDP's 1994 report underscores a shift from "a pattern of wars between states to wars within states." Of the 82 armed conflicts between 1989 and 1992, only three were between states. "Although often cast in ethnic divisions, many have a political or economic character," states the report. Meanwhile, global military spending in 1992 was $815 billion ($725 billion of which corresponded to the rich Northern countries), a figure equal to the combined income of 49 per cent of the world's people in that same year. By 2015, military spending worldwide had more than doubled, to nearly $1.7 trillion.

The period of worldwide political instability we face began in the late twentieth century. It includes civil wars in the former Yugoslavia and in numerous African countries, simmering social conflict in Latin America and Asia, major transnational wars in the Middle East, and endemic civil disturbances, sometimes low-key and sometimes high-profile, in Los Angeles, Paris, Bonn, Athens, and most metropoles of the Northern countries. Uncertain survival and the insecurities posed by global capitalism induce diverse forms of fundamentalism, localism, nationalism, and racial and ethnic conflict.

As the worldwide ruling class, the transnational bourgeoisie has thrust humanity into a crisis of civilization. Social life under global capitalism is increasingly dehumanizing and devoid of any ethical content. But our crisis is deeper: We face a *species crisis*. As many analysts have pointed out, well-known structural contradictions that Marx analyzed a century ago, such as overaccumulation, underconsumption, and the tendency toward stagnation, are exacerbated by globalization. However, while these "classic" contradictions cause financial turmoil, social crisis, and cultural decadence, new contradictions associated with twenty-first century capitalism – namely, the incompatibility of the reproduction of both capital *and* nature – is leading to an ecological holocaust that threatens the survival of our species and of life itself on our planet.

Ninth, stated in highly simplified terms, much of the left worldwide is split between two camps.

One group is so overwhelmed by the power of global capitalism that it does not see any alternative to participation through trying to negotiate the best deal possible. This camp searches for some new variant of social democracy and redistributive justice that could become operant in the new world order. It therefore proposes diverse sorts of global Keynesianism that do not challenge the logic of capitalism itself, and tends toward a political pragmatism.

The other group views global capitalism and its costs – including its very tendency toward the destruction of our species – as unacceptably high, so much so that it must be resisted and rejected. However, *it has not worked out a coherent socialist alternative* to the transnational phase of capitalism.

We see this strategic dividing line in the Latin American, African, and Asian left, as well as in the North and among left and socialist groups attempting a renewal in the former Soviet bloc countries. For instance, this was the fundamental underlying issue that ultimately led to formal splits in the 1990s and early twenty-first century in a number of Latin American leftist organizations, including the Sandinista National Liberation Front (FSLN) in Nicaragua and the Farabundo Marti National Liberation Front (FMLN) in El Salvador. It also led to the fracturing of the Philippine left, the Greek left, the African National Congress coalition in South Africa, leftist parties in the European Union, and so on (although care must be taken to neither simplify complex issues nor to draw broad generalizations from specific experiences).

My own view is that we should harbor no illusions that global capitalism can be tamed or democratized. This does not mean that we should not struggle for reform within capitalism, but that all such struggle should be encapsulated in a broader strategy and program for revolution against capitalism. Globalization places enormous constraints on popular struggles and social change in any one country or region. The most urgent task is therefore to develop solutions to the plight of humanity under a savage capitalism liberated from the constraints that could earlier be imposed on it through the nation-state.

An alternative to global capitalism must therefore be a *transnational* popular project. The transnational bourgeoisie is conscious of its transnationality, is organized transnationally, and operates globally. Many have argued that the nation-state is still the fulcrum of political activity for the foreseeable future. But it is *not* the fulcrum of the political activity of this global elite. The popular mass of humanity must develop a *transnational* class consciousness and a concomitant global political protagonism and strategies that link the local to the national, and the national to the global.

A transnational counter-hegemonic project requires the development of concrete and viable programmatic alternatives. For instance, in the post-apartheid period, the South African Communist Party adopted and internationally popularized a strategy of seeking to "roll back" the market through the decommodification of key areas of South African society, not as an end in itself, but as part of a broader struggle for socialism. Although it later abandoned this strategy, the World Social Forum, which brings together in its annual meetings representatives from thousands of popular social change organizations from around the world, has placed this struggle for reclaiming the global commons at the center of its agenda. The contradictions of global capitalism open new possibilities as well as enormous challenges for a popular alternative. Without their own viable socioeconomic model, popular sectors run the risk of political stagnation under the hegemony of the transnational elite. Even worse, if they come to occupy governments, they may be reduced to administering the crises of neoliberalism, with a consequent loss of legitimacy. In many important respects, this is precisely what happened to several of the leftist governments that came to power in Latin America in the early twenty-first century, such as in Brazil under the Workers Party. In such a scenario, the hegemonic view that there is no popular alternative to global capitalism becomes reinforced, leading to resignation and demobilization among popular sectors and betrayal of obligations among intellectuals and leaders.

The "race to the bottom" – the worldwide downward leveling of living conditions and the gradual equalization of life conditions in North and South – creates fertile objective conditions for the development of transnational social movements and political projects. The communications revolution has facilitated global elite communications, but it can also assist global coordination among popular classes. Examples include the creative use that the Zapatistas in Mexico made of the internet in the years following their 1994 uprising; during the Arab Spring that started in 2010; and with regard to the Occupy Wall Street Movement in the United States of 2011. The formation of the World Social Forum in 2001 marked one turning point in the transnational coordination of national and regional struggles, despite all its shortcomings.

A transnational counter-hegemonic project would not entail resisting globalization. Alas, we cannot simply demand that historic processes be halted to conform to our wishes, and would do better to understand how we may influence and redirect those processes. Instead, we must try to convert it into a "globalization from below." Such a process would have to address from the bottom up the deep racial/ethnic dimensions of global inequality, starting from the premise that, although racism and ethnic and religious conflicts rest on real material fears among groups whose survival is under threat, they take on cultural, ideological and political dynamics of their own which must be challenged and countered in the programs and the practice of counter-hegemony. A counter-hegemonic project will have to be thoroughly imbued with a gender-equality approach, in practice and in content. It will also require alternative forms of democratic practice within popular organizations (trade unions, social movements, etc.), within political parties, and – wherever the formal state apparatus is captured, through elections or other means – within state institutions.

New egalitarian practices must eschew traditional hierarchical and authoritarian forms of social intercourse and bureaucratic authority relations, and overcome personality cults, centralized decision-making, and other such traditional practices. The flow of authority and decision-making in new social and political practices within any counter-hegemonic bloc must be from the bottom up, not from the top down. Transnational political protagonism among popular classes means developing a transnational protagonism at the mass, grassroots level. This transnationalized participatory democracy must go well beyond the old "internationalism" of political leaders and bureaucrats, and beyond the paternalistic forms of Northern "solidarity" with the South.

More than prolonged mass misery and social conflict is at stake: at stake is the very survival of our species. A democratic socialism founded on a popular democracy may be humanity's "last best hope."

Global capitalism, migration labor, and the struggle for justice

First published in *Class, Race and Corporate Power*, 2014

In recent years the international media is full of stories on the rising tide of migrant workers in the global system, their struggles, trials and tribulations, and the widespread repression and hostility they face everywhere from authoritarian states and racist publics. Some of the stories from around the world that have made headlines are: the crisis, largely contrived, of Latin American child migration and hysteria over a so-called "border invasion" in the United States; the rising tide of racist violence against migrant workers in North America, Europe, Israel, and elsewhere; the tragedy of thousands of people from Africa and the Middle East drowning in the Mediterranean as they attempt to reach Europe; pogroms against southern African immigrant workers in South African cities; the death by heat stroke and work accidents of thousands of South Asian workers in Qatar as the toil to construct World Cup stadiums; and the suicide of dozens of internal immigrant workers in China's coastal sweatshops, among others. Everywhere, borders are militarized, states are stepping up repressive anti-immigrant controls, and native publics are turning immigrants into scapegoats for the spiraling crisis of global capitalism. Yet everywhere, there is the rise of migrant justice movements and workers' fightbacks in which immigrant workers play a pivotal and often leading role.

The massive displacement and primitive accumulation unleashed by capitalist globalization as well as state and "private" violence has resulted in a virtually inexhaustible migrant labor reserve for the global economy. In turn, repressive state controls over migrant labor have several functions for the system. First, state repression and criminalization of undocumented migration makes them vulnerable and deportable, and therefore subject to conditions of super-exploitation, super-control, and hyper-surveillance. Second, anti-immigrant repressive apparatuses and social control systems are themselves ever more important sources of accumulation, ranging from private, for-profit immigrant detention centers to the militarization of borders, and the purchase by states of military hardware and systems of surveillance. Third, the anti-immigrant policies associated with repressive state apparatuses help turn attention away from the crisis of global capitalism among more privileged sectors of the working classes, such as middle layers in the global South or white workers in the North, and convert immigrant workers into scapegoats for the crisis, thus deflecting attention from the root causes of the crisis and undermining working-class unity.

The story of migrant labor in the twenty-first century is therefore central to that of the new global capitalism and to that of the struggles of the global working class for justice and emancipation. This essay will reflect on a portion of this story, with a particular focus on the structural and historical underpinnings of the phenomenon of migrant labor in the new global capitalist system, and on the United States as an illustration of the larger worldwide condition of migration and migrant justice.

Capitalism, the world labor market, and migration/immigration

Perhaps the most pressing problem the capitalist system faces is how to secure a politically and economically suitable supply of labor. But what does securing "suitable" labor mean? In the first place, it means uprooting people from their land and other means of livelihood, or what is known as their *primitive accumulation*, so that they have no choice but to work for capital if they want to survive. Second, it means generating a large enough pool of labor that this pool can be dipped into as needed; later, these same workers can be disposed of when not needed. Third, it means generating the means and conditions to deploy that labor wherever it is needed around the world. Finally, it means developing systems of repression and ideological hegemony to assure that workers are tightly controlled, disorganized, disciplined, and obedient.

Central to the formation of the world capitalist system was the creation of a world market in labor. Securing this politically and economically suitable labor supply has historically been a key function of colonialism and imperialism. Over the past five centuries of world capitalism, dominant groups have created and constantly recreated this market through the most violent and destructive processes imaginable. The formation of a world market in labor has involved such mechanisms as:

- The kidnapping and forced removal of some twenty million Africans to the New World.
- The internal transfer in this New World of tens of millions of indigenous people.
- The displacement from their lands of millions of European peasants by the forces of capitalist expansion and their migration around the world as laborers.
- The so-called second slavery from the 1870s into the 1930s of millions of "coolie" laborers from India and China who, under the weight of colonialism, found themselves displaced, dispossessed, and swept up by international labor recruiters by hook and crook to build railroads or work plantations in Africa, Asia, and the Western hemisphere.

This creation of a world labor market is simultaneously the history of migration, and the history of the racialization of global class relations through the creation by dominant groups of racial and ethnic hierarchies within the labor pools that the system has brought into being and sustained over the 500 years of its existence. If migration/immigration has thus been central to the creation of the world capitalist system, today it is just as crucial to the reproduction of the new global capitalism. However, under capitalist globalization, a new global immigrant labor supply system has come to replace earlier direct colonial and racial caste controls over labor worldwide. There is a new global working class that labors in the factories, farms, commercial establishments, and offices of the global economy. This new working class faces conditions of precariousness, is predominantly female, and, for the purposes of this article, is increasingly based on immigrant labor.

The rise of new systems of transnational labor mobility and recruitment have made it possible for dominant groups around the world to reorganize labor markets and recruit transient labor forces that are disenfranchised and easy to control. The latter decades of the twentieth century began a period of massive new migrations worldwide. In 1960, there were some 75 million immigrant workers worldwide; in 1980, there were 100 million. According to the low-end estimate of the United Nations, this figure then shot up to some

200 million immigrant workers worldwide in 2005 – double the figure from 1980. The International Labor Organization then put the figure for 2014 at 232 million. These figures do not account for the tens of millions of Chinese who have migrated from the interior of China to the coastal cities to work in the industrial sweatshops that now serve as the leading workshop of the world, and who in practice constitute an immigrant workforce as a result of Chinese internal pass and residency laws (known as the *hukou* system).

Historically, migrant labor has flowed from the colonized regions to the metropolitan countries. Today, major transnational migrant flows are still from Latin America and Asia into North America, from Africa, the Middle East and South Asia into Europe, and so on – that is, from the traditional peripheries to the traditional cores of the world capitalist system. However, that pattern is rapidly changing. Now we see that major axes of accumulation in the global economy attract immigrant labor from neighboring regions. Intense transnational corporate activity, wherever it takes place in the new global economy – from the factories along China's southern coastal belt, to the South African mines and farms, the Middle East oil meccas, and Costa Rica's service industry – becomes a magnet for immigrant workers. And wherever these workers end up, they face the same conditions: relegation to low-paid, low-status jobs, the denial of labor rights, political disenfranchisement, state repression, racism, bigotry, and nativism.

Nicaraguans migrate to Costa Rica; Bolivians to Argentina; Peruvians to Chile; Southern and Central Africans to South Africa; Indians, Pakistanis, and Sri Lankans to the Middle East oil producers; Indonesians to Malaysia; and Myanma to Thailand. Israel has recently become a major importer of transnational migrant labor from Asia and North Africa. (This is a particularly attractive option for Israel because it does away with the need for politically troublesome Palestinian labor.) Over 300,000 immigrant workers from Thailand, China, Nepal, and Sri Lanka now form the predominant labor force in Israeli agribusiness in the same way as Mexican and Central American immigrant labor does in U.S. agribusiness, and under the same precarious conditions of super-exploitation and discrimination. The Philippines presents an extreme case: the Philippine government and private recruitment firms organize the export of Philippine workers to some 200 countries around the world. These labor migrations are not voluntary in the sense that the structural violence of the system is what forces people to migrate. It is therefore important to see transnational immigrant labor as a form of *coerced* labor.

Once they arrive at their destinations, undocumented immigrants join the ranks of a super-exploitable labor force available for transnational corporations, local employers, and native middle classes. It is often said that while capital has torn down national barriers to its global mobility and it is now free to cross borders at will – and this is quite true – it is also true that labor is *globally* mobile, not it the sense that it can freely cross borders, but in the sense that in practice the structural conditions of capitalist globalization not only make possible but actually facilitate the worldwide deployment of migrant labor as needed by capital worldwide. Migrant workers are globally mobile, but under conditions of extreme repressive control over their movement and over their very existence. Borders and the international state system are essential for capitalist domination over workers and the creation and reproduction of a global reserve army of migrant workers.

Globalization and the creation of "immigrant labor"

Global capitalism is characterized by several fundamental changes in the capitalist system that have implications for how we understand the role of labor and the struggle for social justice. Among these changes is the rise of truly transnational capital and the integration of every country into the new system of globalized production, finances, and services, and the rise of a transnational capitalist class (TCC). The TCC is a new class group grounded in global over local or national circuits of accumulation and which, together with transnationally oriented state bureaucrats and politicians, is the manifest agent of capitalist globalization.

Capital responded to the worldwide structural crisis of the 1970s by "going global" in an attempt to break through the constraints that the nation-state – that is, the working and popular classes operating at the nation-state level – placed on accumulation. These working and popular classes were unwilling to shoulder the burden of the crisis, and so long as they could pressure states to place constraints on capital, they could sustain a standoff with capital that generated "stagflation," a decline in profits, and a growing political and ideological crisis of hegemony. In response, dominant groups called for a vast restructuring of world capitalism. With the election of Ronald Reagan in the United States and Margaret Thatcher in Britain, they launched the "neoliberal counter-revolution" as an offensive against working and popular classes everywhere, involving the dismantling of developmentalist, socialist, and redistributive projects.

The global mobility of capital associated with globalization allowed the TCC to break free of nation-state constraints to accumulation. It has restructured the world economy, fragmented production and the labor process, and altered the correlation of class and social forces in its favor, at least in the momentary historic conjuncture of the late twentieth and early twenty-first centuries. Free-trade agreements and neoliberal policies have displaced hundreds of millions of people around the world and generated a vast pool of under- and unemployed labor thrown into the global jobs market.

As a result, the TCC has been able to forge a new capital–labor relation based on the "flexibilization" or "Walmartization" of labor. Under this new modality of flexible labor, workers no longer enjoy the protection of state regulation of the capital–labor relation. They face conditions of de-unionization and are informalized, casualized, part-time, on short-term contracts, and temporary. Workers have increasingly become a commodified input to production just like any other raw material. They can be hired and fired at will and enjoy no stability, becoming what many are now referring to as the new "precariat": the proletariat that labors under conditions of permanent insecurity and precariousness. Crucial to the new labor relations of global capitalism is the elimination of any reciprocity between capital and labor; capital bears no responsibility for the social reproduction of labor, on the one hand, and on the other, the state abandons redistributive policies that recirculate value back to labor in the form of the social wages. Instead, it subsidizes capital.

These new class relations of global capitalism have in part been made possible by capital's newfound mobility, and in part by the dramatic expansion of the global surplus population – that portion who are marginalized and locked out of productive participation in the capitalist economy, and who constitute some one-third of humanity. This mass of "supernumeraries" is of no *direct* use to capital. However, in the larger picture, such surplus labor is crucial to global capitalism insofar as it places downward pressure on wages everywhere, especially to the extent that global labor markets can be tapped and labor can be mobilized throughout the global economy. This allows transnational capital to impose discipline over those who remain active in the labor market.

There is a broad social and political base, therefore, for the maintenance of flexible, super-controlled, and super-exploited immigrant labor pools. The system cannot function without them. But if global capital needs the labor power of transnational migrants, the human beings who own this labor power must be tightly controlled, given the special oppression and dehumanization involved in extracting their labor power as non-citizen immigrant workers. The state must play a balancing act by finding a formula for providing a stable supply of cheap labor to employers while exercising ever greater state control over immigrants. The dilemma (and the contradiction) for capital, dominant groups, and the affluent and privileged strata becomes how to assure a steady supply of immigrant labor while at the same time promoting anti-immigrant practices and ideologies. The instruments for achieving the dual goals of super-exploitability and super-controllability are: 1) the division of the working class into immigrant and citizen, and 2) a special oppression immigrant workers, often involving racialization and criminalization. Racialization is a critical tool to the rule of capital in the politics of domination.

Criminalization and militarization increasingly drive underground undocumented immigrants around the world. There, in the quest for survival, they become vulnerable to intermediaries such as gangs, drug traffickers, sexual exploiters, shady temporary labor agencies, and unscrupulous employers. The array of state and other institutional controls over immigrants further drives down informal and black-market wages and working and living conditions, while giving employers an ever-freer hand. At the same time, borders must be militarized to be effective instruments for regulating and controlling the supply of immigrant labor. By the end of the twentieth century, the U.S.–Mexico border, for instance, was already one of the most militarized stretches of land in the world, with ten guards for every mile for the length of the 2,000-mile border. Many stretches along the frontier are akin to a war zone. U.S. president

Donald Trump's fanatical campaign to "build the wall" was distinct only in rhetoric from the border militarization pursued by his predecessors, Democratic and Republican alike.

The globalization of production, finances, and services has increased transnational capital's ability to fragment labor markets in each locale, and to create and reproduce new forms of labor market segmentation at the transborder level. This worldwide deployment of migrant labor occurs through institutional arrangements: states create "immigrant labor" as a distinct juridical category of labor. The global working class thus becomes divided between "citizen" and "immigrant" labor. This is a major new axis of inequality worldwide. The super-exploitation of a migrant workforce would not be possible if that workforce had the same civil, political, and labor rights as citizens, and if it did not face the insecurities and vulnerabilities of being undocumented or "illegal." State controls over immigrant labor are intended not to *prevent* but to *control* the transnational movement of labor and to lock that labor into permanent insecurity and vulnerability. The creation of these distinct categories replaces earlier direct colonial and racial caste controls over labor worldwide.

In this age of globalization, the creation of two distinct categories of labor around the world – "immigrant" and "citizen" – constitutes a new rigid caste system that has become central to the global economy and worldwide capital accumulation. Reproducing the division of workers into immigrants and citizens requires contradictory practices on the part of states. The state must provide capital with immigrant labor. However, it must also legitimate the mechanisms of control and surveillance and to turn native against immigrant labor. It does this through its ideological activities, generating a nationalist hysteria by propagating such images as "out-of-control-borders" and "invasions of illegal immigrants". Granting full citizenship rights to the hundreds of millions of immigrants and their families would undermine the division of the global working class into immigrants and citizens, which would weaken capital's ability to divide and exploit the global working class. The struggle of migrant workers is therefore at the cutting edge of popular movements worldwide against the depredations of global capitalism, and is central to the struggle of the global working class.

In the era of globalization, states practice a "revolving door" function, opening and shutting the flow of immigration in accordance with the flux of national politics and the needs of capital accumulation during distinct periods. Immigrants are sucked up when their labor is needed, and then spat out when they become superfluous or potentially destabilizing to the system. The condition of *deportable* must be created and then reproduced – periodically refreshed with new waves of "illegal" immigrants – since that condition assures the ability to super-exploit labor with impunity and to dispose of it without consequences should it become unruly or unnecessary. Driving immigrant labor deeper underground and absolving the state and employers of any commitment to the social reproduction of this labor allows for its maximum exploitation together with its disposal when necessary.

Labor supply through transnational migration constitutes the *export of commodified human beings*. This commodification goes beyond the more limited concept first developed by Marx, in which the worker's *labor power* is sold to capital as a commodity. To Marx, we must add Foucauldian insights: in particular, recognition that control reaches beyond the productive structure, beyond consumption and social relations, to *encompass the body itself* (hence "biopolitics"). In the classical Marxist construct, the worker faces alienation and exploitation during the time they sell this commodity to capital, that is, during the work shift. In between this regularized sale of labor power they are not a commodity but an alienated human being, "free" to rest and replenish in the sphere of social reproduction.

In its archetypical form, the new migrant worker as a mobile input for globalized circuits of accumulation is not just selling commodified labor during the time they are working; *the whole body becomes a commodity*, mobilized and supplied in the same way as are raw materials, money, intermediate goods, and other inputs. It is, after all, the whole body that must migrate and insert itself into the global accumulation circuits as immigrant labor. Hence, even when each regular sale of labor power concludes – i.e., after each work period – the worker is not "free" to rest and replenish as in the traditional Marxist analysis of labor and capital. This is because they remain *immigrant/undocumented labor* 24 hours a day. They are therefore unable to engage in the "normal" channels of rest and social reproduction, due to the whole set of institutional exclusions, state controls, racialized discrimination, xenophobia, and oppression that the undocumented immigrant worker experiences in the larger social milieu. The worldwide immigrant labor regime becomes the very epitome of transnational capital's naked domination in the age of globalization.

In the United States and Europe, and in several countries in Latin America and Asia, immigrants have been denied access to basic social services and benefits, that is, to the social wage. Immigrant workers in these countries are responsible for their own maintenance and reproduction, and – through remittances – for their family members abroad. This makes immigrant labor cheap and flexible for capital *and also* costless for the state compared to native-born labor. *Immigrant workers become the archetype of the new global class relations: the quintessential workforce of global capitalism.* They are yanked out of relations of reciprocity rooted in social and political communities that have historically been institutionalized in nation-states. As well, immigrant workers send billions of dollars home to their families and communities. These monies make possible social reproduction in home countries and thus alleviate pressures that may otherwise generate political crises, and allow receiving families to consume goods made in the Global Factory and distributed in the Global Mall. These transnationally recycled wages also enter the financial system and help balance state budgets and achieve macroeconomic stability.

Anti-immigrant politics and the immigrant justice movement: the case of the United States

As the United States has led the way in globalization, it has also led the way in the construction of a new transient labor system. During the 1980s, eight million Latin American migrants arrived in the United States as globalization, neoliberalism and global labor-market restructuring induced a wave of outmigration from Latin America. This was nearly equal to the total figure of European immigrants who arrived on U.S. shores during the first decades of the twentieth century and made Latin America the principal origin of migration into the United States. Some 36 million immigrant workers were in the United States in 2010, at least 20 million of them from Latin America.

Right-wing politicians, law-enforcement agents, and neo-fascist anti-immigrant movements may intentionally generate racist hostility toward Latinos and other immigrants. The U.S. Southern Command has gone so far as to frame migration as a national security threat, calling it – in the words of Gen. John Kelly, who at the time was commander of U.S. military forces operating throughout Latin America – a "crime–terror convergence." Yet this anti-immigrant hostility may also be the effect of the structural and legal–institutional subordination of immigrant workers and their communities, or simply an unintended (although not necessarily unwelcomed) byproduct of the state's coercive policies. Embodied in this structural condition is the rise and the ongoing re-composition of an internally stratified global working class controlled by political borders, state repression, criminalization, and militarization. The United States's war on immigrants has fed hate crimes against immigrant workers and hostility toward Latino and other immigrant communities. This war has included an escalation of workplace and community raids; detentions and deportations; racial profiling; new surveillance systems (such as e-Verify); police abuse; and so forth.

The activities of the American Legislative Exchange Council (ALEC), expose the inner connections between corporate interests, the state, militarization and policing, and anti-immigrant and other neo-fascist tendencies in civil society. ALEC brings together state and federal elected officials and law enforcement and criminal justice system representatives with some 200 of the most powerful transnational corporations. Among these are AT&T, Coca-Cola, ExxonMobil, Pfizer, Kraft Heinz, Walmart, Bank of America, Microsoft, Nestlé, AstraZeneca, Dow Chemical, Sony, and Koch Industries – this latter being one of the biggest ALEC funders. ALEC develops legislative initiatives that advance the transnational corporate agenda, hammering out in its gatherings draft bills on criminal justice, anti-unionization, tax reform, financial and environmental deregulation, and related topics. These bills are then tabled by state and local elected officials associated with ALEC. They have included the notorious "three strikes law" that mandates 25-years-to-life sentences for those committing a third offense (even for minor drug possession), and "truth in sentencing," which requires people to serve all their time with no chance of parole.

State assemblyman Russell Pearce, an ALEC board member, first introduced the notorious anti-immigrant law SB1070 into the state legislature. In 2009, ALEC members including Pearce and representatives from the Corrections Corporation of America (CCA), the largest private prison operator in the United States, drafted a model anti-immigrant law. Pearce then introduced the bill into the Arizona legislature with the support of 36 co-sponsors, thirty of whom received campaign contributions from CCA lobbyists as well as from lobbyists for two other private prison companies, GEO Group and Management & Training Corporation. In 2010, the bill was signed by Arizona governor Jan Brewer, who herself has close ties to the CCA and ALEC. The CCA has received lucrative contracts to run immigrant detention centers in Arizona. SB1070 legalized racial profiling by instructing state law-enforcement agents to detain and question anyone who appeared to be undocumented, and authorizing anyone to sue police who failed to do so, requiring in effect everyone to carry proof of citizenship or legal residence at all times. Among other stipulations, it also required teachers to compile lists of suspected immigrant children, and directed emergency rooms and social service agencies to deny care to those who cannot prove citizenship or legal residence.

Although some of the most draconian provisions were struck down later by federal courts, the Arizona law became a model for "copycat" legislation passed in five other states and introduced in several dozen more. The magazine *Mother Jones* built a database of hundreds of repressive local- and state-level anti-immigrant laws introduced around the U.S. in the wake of SB1070, including 164 such laws passed by state legislatures in 2010 and 2011 alone. The database also uncovered the extensive interlocking of far-right organizations comprising the anti-immigrant movement, other neo-fascist organizations in civil society, government agencies and elected officials (local and federal), politicians, and corporate and foundation funders, lobbyists, and activists.

Immigrant labor is extremely profitable for the transnational corporate economy in a double sense. First, it is highly vulnerable labor, forced to exist semi-underground; it is *deportable*, and therefore super-exploitable. Second, criminalizing undocumented immigrants and militarizing their control not only reproduces these conditions of vulnerability, but also generates vast new opportunities for accumulation. The private immigrant detention complex is a boom industry. Undocumented immigrants constitute the fastest-growing sector of the U.S. prison population as they are detained in private detention centers and deported by private companies contracted out by the U.S. state. As of 2010, there were 270 immigration detention centers that, on any given day, were caging over 30,000 immigrants and annually locking up some 400,000 individuals. Compare this to just a few dozen people in immigrant detention each day prior to the 1980s – that is, prior to the launching of capitalist globalization and the new transnational systems of labor recruitment and control associated with it.

Under the presidency of Barack Obama, more immigrants were detained and deported than at any time in the previous half-century. Detentions and deportations then escalated further under the Trump and Biden presidencies, continuing the pattern that began in the 1980s. Some detention centers housed entire families, so that children were behind bars with their parents. Since detainment facilities and deportation logistics are subcontracted to private companies, capital has a vested interest in the criminalization of immigrants and in the militarization of control over immigrants – and more broadly, therefore, a vested interest in contributing to the neo-fascist anti-immigrant movement.

A month after SB1070 became law, Wayne Calabrese, the president of GEO Group, held a conference call with investors and explained his company's aspirations. "Opportunities at the federal level are going to continue apace as a result of what's happening," he said, referring to the Arizona law. "Those people coming across the border being caught are going to have to be detained and that to me at least suggests there's going to be enhanced opportunities for what we do." The 2005 annual report of the CCA stated with regard to the profit-making opportunities opened up by the prison-industrial complex: "Our growth is generally dependent upon our ability to obtain new contracts to develop and manage new correctional and detention facilities ... The demand for our facilities and services could be adversely affected by the relaxation of enforcement efforts, leniency in conviction and sentencing practices or through the decriminalization of certain activities that are currently proscribed by our criminal laws." The day after Donald Trump's November 2016 electoral victory, the CCA stock price soared 40 per cent, a response to Trump's promise to deport millions of immigrants.

By the second decade of the twenty-first century, every year over 350,000 immigrants were going through privately run prisons for the undocumented and record numbers were being deported, even though the absolute number of immigrants had declined. The United States spends more on immigration enforcement than all other enforcement activities of the federal government combined, including the FBI, the Drug Enforcement Administration, and the Bureau of Alcohol, Tobacco, Firearms and Explosives.

The immigrant justice movement

As anti-immigrant scapegoating and oppression heightened in the latter part of the twentieth century, so too did resistance on the part of immigrants and their supporters, alongside labor struggles in which immigrant workers have played an ever more prominent role. In the United States, the immigrant justice movement dates back decades – but it exploded into mass protests in the spring of 2006. This was triggered by the introduction in the U.S. Senate of a draconian piece of draft legislation, known as the Sensenbrenner bill for the name of the sponsoring senator, that would have criminalized undocumented immigrants and their supporters. These mass protests in the spring of 2006 helped defeat the Sensenbrenner bill but also sparked an escalation of state repression and racist nativism and fueled the neo-fascist anti-immigrant movement. The backlash has involved, among other things, stepped-up raids on immigrant workplaces and communities, mass deportations, an increase in the number of federal immigration enforcement agents, the deputizing of local police forces as enforcement agents, the further militarization of the U.S.–Mexico border, anti-immigrant hysteria in the mass media, and the introduction at the local, state, and federal levels of a slew of discriminatory anti-immigrant legislative initiatives.

In the face of what can only be described as a terror campaign against immigrant communities, a split occurred. In simplified terms, the more "moderate" or liberal wing of the leadership pursued a strategy of seeking allies in the halls of power and limiting mass mobilization to a pressure mechanism on elites to open up space at the table for the Latino establishment. The more radical, grassroots-oriented wing insisted on building a mass movement for immigrant rights and social justice from the ground up, framing the issue as a working-class struggle. The liberal camp sought allies in Congress, among the Democrats, organized labor, and mainstream civil rights and public advocacy organizations, to negotiate more favorable immigrant reform legislation. This camp was willing to sacrifice the interests of some immigrants in order to win concessions from mainstream allies, such as forsaking full legalization for all immigrants in exchange for dubious "paths to citizenship," and to compromise over such issues such as "guest workers programs," which have been condemned as indentured servitude and have been shown to place the labor movement in a more vulnerable position. The radical grassroots camp, in contrast, insisted on prioritizing a permanent mass movement from below that subordinated alliances with liberals to the interests of the disenfranchised majority of immigrant workers and their families. This camp also insisted on the need to link the immigrant rights movement more openly and closely with other popular, labor, and resistance struggles for global justice around the world.

These distinct strategies represent, in the broader analysis, two different class projects within the multi-class community of immigrants and their supporters: the former, those middle-class strata who aspire to remove racist and legal impediments to their own class status; the latter, a mass immigrant working class that faces not just ethnic oppression and legal discrimination, but also the acute labor exploitation and survival struggles imposed on them by a rapacious global capitalism. This dividing line was played out from 2006 until 2016 in a succession of "comprehensive immigration reform" bills that were introduced into Congress. Although none passed, almost all of them involved a greatly expanded militarization of the border ("securing the border"), the expansion of "guest worker" programs, and the introduction and expansion of other repressive state controls over immigrant communities and work centers, in exchange for extremely limited concessions with regard to the legalization of a small portion of the more than 12 million undocumented immigrants.

While Democratic Party and Latino establishment organizations and leaders pushed the legal reform strategy, the grassroots immigrant justice movement expanded struggles on numerous fronts. Immigrant workers' centers sprang up in every locale across the United States where such workers were present, and many of them became organized into the National Day Labor Organizing Committee and the National Domestic Workers

Alliance. The Binational Front of Indigenous Organizations worked transnationally among immigrant-sending communities in Mexico and immigrant workers' communities in the United States. The "Dignity Campaign" was a loose coalition of local and national immigrant justice and fair-trade organizations, who proposed alternatives to immigrant reform legislation that stressed "border enforcement" and criminalization of immigrant communities. Instead, they encouraged the movement to see immigration in the global context and to draw out the connections between trade policies, displacement, and migration.

Both the immigrant justice struggle and the anti-immigrant backlash came together in the spring and summer of 2014 in the so-called "invasion" of Central American children, a fabricated story and a classic example of how a "moral panic" is generated by the moral entrepreneurs of dominant groups and the state, and manipulated from above. As Bacon has shown, the "story" began when U.S. immigration officials gave photos showing children in immigration detention centers to a media outlet in Texas associated with the Tea Party (an extreme-right wing faction of the U.S. Republican Party). This appears to have been a well-planned strategy to whip up a "moral panic," to put the immigrant justice movement on the defensive, to undermine immigration reform in Congress, and above all to legitimate a new spiral of militarization and criminalization.

Fanned by propaganda from the anti-immigrant movement, for several months the mainstream media bombarded the public with sensationalist stories of an invasion by Central American children. These provocative accounts provided no context with regard to the roots of such migration in the long history of U.S. intervention in the region or the devastation caused by U.S. counterinsurgency wars. Nor did they mention how these wars were followed by neoliberal free-trade policies and renewed militarization that have left the region in economic devastation, spreading social violence and despair. The media also ignored that there was nothing "new" about the surge; such migration had been taking place for years and had been steadily increasing since 2000. The "moral panic" gave anti-immigrant forces the opportunity to stage some of the most vicious racist public demonstrations in recent years.

The election of the openly racist and anti-immigrant Donald

Trump to the presidency in 2016 resulted in a sharp escalation of anti-immigrant hysteria. This was part of the Trump regime's strategy to scapegoat immigrants for the capitalist crisis. But beyond mere scapegoating, the criminalization of immigrants, the increase in raids and detentions, and the "build the wall" rhetoric were part of a larger strategy to disarticulate political organization and resistance among immigrant communities. It was not surprising that, as Trump took office, the wave of detentions and deportation of immigrants from Mexico and Central America targeted labor and community activists among the undocumented immigrant community. Despite a softer rhetoric, the Biden government that succeeded Trump continued these policies. U.S. rulers appeared to be pushing forward with the effort to replace the system of super-exploitation of undocumented immigrant labor with a mass "guest worker program" that would be more efficient in combining super-exploitation with super-control. Indeed, while the detention and deportation of undocumented immigrant workers in California escalated in the second decade of the twenty-first century, the use of "guest workers" in that state's $47 billion agricultural industry increased by 500 per cent from 2011 to 2017.

Conclusions: Working-class hegemony, global citizenship, and universal human rights

Criminalization and militarized control over immigrant labor reflects a broader militarization of the global economy. Beyond the United States, major sectors of the TCC are becoming dependent on local, regional, and global violence, conflict, and inequalities. In fact, they push for such conflict through their influence on states and in political and cultural systems. This militarized accumulation is characteristic of the entire global economy. We are increasingly living in a global war economy, and certain countries, such as the United States and Israel, are key gears in this machinery. Militarized accumulation to control and contain the downtrodden and marginalized, and to sustain accumulation in the face of crisis, feeds into fascist political tendencies – to a twenty-first century fascism. A key element of this global war economy is the transnational migrant detention and repression complex.

A mass immigrant rights movement is at the cutting edge of the struggle against transnational corporate exploitation. Granting full citizenship rights to the hundreds of millions of immigrants around the world would undermine the division of the global working class into immigrants and citizens. That division is a central component of the new class relations of global capitalism, predicated on a casualized and "flexible" mass of workers who can be hired and fired at will, are de-unionized, and face precarious work conditions, job instability, a rollback of benefits, and downward pressures on wages.

The strategic challenge of the immigrant justice movement, in the United States as elsewhere, is how to achieve the hegemony of the mass worker base within the movement. The expanding crisis of global capitalism opens up grave dangers – for immigrants and for all of humanity – but also creates opportunities. It is not to the political parties of the status quo (e.g., the Democratic Party in the United States), to the TCC, or to the halls of establishment power, but to the mass base of this movement – the communities of poor immigrant workers and their families who swell the cities and rural towns of the world – to whom we must turn to reverse the anti-immigrant onslaught, which, we must be clear, is a systematic attack on the entire working class.

More broadly – and although this idea might clash with progressives or even socialists who for decades have fought for citizenship rights for all – the whole notion of *national* citizenship needs to be questioned. Borders are not in the interests of the global working class; they should be torn down. So long as the rights we associate with citizenship are seen to adhere to a limited group of people who belong to a nation, there will always be those who fall outside of the nation and who are excluded from these rights; there will always be *Others*. We must consider citizenship rights as universal human rights for all people who, for whatever reason, happen to reside in a particular territory. We must replace the whole concept of *national* citizenship with that of *global* citizenship. This is a truly revolutionary rallying cry. And it is the only one that can assure justice and equality for all.

Global capitalism and the restructuring of education

Producing global economy workers and suppressing critical thinking

First published in *Social Justice*, 2017

In recent decades, world capitalism has been undergoing a process of *capitalist globalization*, or profound restructuring and expansion. What type of "human capital" does the emerging global capitalist system require to function (which is to say, for capital accumulation to overcome the technical and political impediments to its continuous expansion)? For one, it needs a cadre of organic intellectuals to do the overall thinking and strategizing for the system, and a small army of technocrats and administrators to resolve problems of system maintenance and development. At the same time, this system needs a very large army of people who will supply nothing but their labor and who are not disposed or equipped to think critically and reflectively on the nature of their existence, or on that of a system sustained by great inequalities and ever more repressive and ubiquitous social control. Finally, it needs a mass of humanity as surplus labor, let us say a few billion people or so, who can serve as a *reserve* supply of manual and other forms of low-skilled and flexible labor in agriculture, industry, and services, who can be carefully controlled at all times, and can be discarded when no longer needed.

What kind of educational system would be able to deliver such a mass of humanity endowed with the skills, knowledge, and mental faculties (or lack thereof) needed to meet these requirements? Certainly, there would be a core of elite centers of education where the organic intellectuals who administer the system and engage in its ongoing design would study and train. Below it would be a tier of educational institutions producing every sort of vocational and technocratic expert, what Robert Reich once referred to as "symbolic analysts" and others as "knowledge workers," meaning that these people would be trained in the use and manipulation of symbols, whether as engineers, computer programmers, scientists, or financial analysts. In exchange for their services and their obedience they would be rewarded with comfortable lifestyles.

Then there would be the 80 per cent, that mass of humanity increasingly precaritized and thrown into the ranks of surplus labor, for which basic numeracy and literacy skills are all that is required in order to supply labor for the system, yet whose potential for critical thinking could pose a serious threat. This tier in the educational system would be quite restricted in its content if not in its provision, serving the dual function of supplying the numeracy, literacy, and technical knowledge necessary to be servile workers while suppressing the development of critical thinking that could contribute to mounting a challenge to global capitalism and punitive social control. In fact, this is just the kind of educational system that the transnational elite has promoted worldwide in recent years.

The trifurcation of humanity: the one per cent, the 20 per cent, and the 80 per cent

On the eve of the 2015 annual World Economic Forum meeting in Davos, Switzerland, an event attended exclusively by the cream of the transnational business, political, and cultural elite (it costs about $40,000 to attend, and at that, one must be invited), the development NGO Oxfam released a report on global inequality, aptly titled *Wealth: Having it All and Wanting More*. The report observed that the wealthiest one per cent of humanity owned 48 per cent of the world's wealth in 2014, up from 44 per cent in 2009, and that under current trends, this one per cent would own more than 50 per cent by the next year.

The obscenity of such concentrations of wealth becomes truly apparent when seen in the context of *expanding inequality*. The report identified the world's richest 80 billionaires among this one per cent, whose wealth *increased* from $1.3 trillion in 2010 to $1.9 trillion in 2014, an increase of $600 billion in just four years, or by *50 per cent* in nominal terms. The wealth of these eighty billionaires was more than all of the wealth owned by the poorer half of the world's population. At the same time, this poorer half of humanity saw its wealth *decrease by 50 per cent* during the same period. In other words, there was a direct transfer of hundreds of billions of dollars from the poorest half of humanity to the richest 80 people on the planet.

While the report characterized such inequality as "simply staggering," it is noteworthy that, according to Oxfam, this polarization of wealth between the poorest half of humanity and the richest eighty people on earth – all but seven of whom are men – actually *accelerated* since the 2008 financial collapse, so it would seem that the crisis has made the rich many times richer and the poor many times more poor. It is similarly worth noting that the world's top billionaires and the one per cent are concentrated in the financial and insurance sector (Warren Buffett and Michael Bloomberg led the way, followed by the likes of George Soros, a Saudi prince, several Russian oligarchs, a Brazilian, and a Colombian). Another major portion of these richest people are concentrated in the pharmaceutical and healthcare sectors, and here Indian and Chinese billionaires lead the way, together with magnates from Turkey, Russia, Switzerland, and elsewhere. And such immense concentrations of wealth translate in manifold ways into political influence: according to Oxfam, in recent years, the financial and pharmaceutical sectors spent close to $1 billion on lobbying in the United States alone.

The Occupy Wall Street movement of 2011–12 brought to worldwide attention the concentration of the world's wealth in the hands of the one per cent with its famous rallying cry, "We are the 99 per cent!" However, an equally, if not more significant division of the world's population with regard to political and sociological analysis is between the better-off 20 per cent of humanity and the remaining 80 per cent. That better-off – if not necessarily outright wealthy – portion's basic material needs are met; it enjoys the fruits of the global cornucopia and generally enjoys conditions of security and stability. This is in sharp contrast to the bottom 80 per cent of the world's people who face escalating poverty, depravation, insecurity, and precariousness. The Oxfam report noted that the richest 20 per cent of humanity owned 94.5 per cent of the world's wealth in 2014, while the remaining 80 per cent had to make do with just 5.5 per cent of that wealth. In other words, the world, in simplified terms, faces a trifurcated structure of the one per cent, the 20 per cent, and the 80 per cent.

The global elite has taken note of these extreme inequalities (as evidenced in the inordinate attention received by French economist Thomas Piketty's 2014 study, *Capital in the Twenty-First Century*) and is concerned that such polarization threatens to undermine growth (read: accumulation) and may lead to instability or even rebellion. But there is little or no discussion among the one per cent about any fundamental redistribution of wealth and power downward; instead, the elite has turned to expanding the mechanisms of ideological and cultural hegemony as well as repression. Both coercive and consensual domination are practiced and constructed in and through educational systems, the media and culture industries, and political and policing systems. The mass of humanity is to be seduced by the promise of petty (and generally banal) consumption and entertainment, backed by the threat of coercion and repression (terror) should dissatisfaction lead to rebellion.

So what type of a worldwide educational system would this one per cent, the global ruling class, presumably attempt to construct in the face of such a trifurcation of humanity? I was asked to ponder just such a question for my participation in a 2015 conference on elite education; to discuss my theory of global capitalism and how a focus on global political economy may shed light on the matter of the worldwide educational system in these neoliberal times. To understand the implications of globalization for elites and power relations worldwide, including global capital's changing needs with regard to educational systems, we must turn to the political economy of global capitalism as a qualitatively new epoch in the ongoing and open-ended evolution of the world capitalist system.

Capitalist globalization and crisis

Capitalism experiences major episodes of crisis about every 40–50 years, as obstacles emerge to ongoing accumulation and profit-making. These are "structural" or "restructuring" crises because the system must be restructured in order to overcome the crisis. As opportunities dry up for capitalists to profitably invest, the system seeks to open up new outlets for surplus capital, typically through violence, whether structural or direct. Structural adjustment programs imposed on the former Third World countries, austerity measures, "free-trade" agreements, and capital flight are examples of structural violence (a recent example was Greece's struggle with the EU-IMF-private banking complex troika). Meanwhile, U.S. wars of intervention in the Middle East, militarization of borders, and construction of prison-industrial complexes are forms of direct violence. Both forms of violence have the simultaneous function of opening up new opportunities for capitalist *expansion* and *control* in the face of stagnation.

Structural crises of capitalism, along with their economic dimension, involve social upheavals, political and military conflict, and ideological and cultural change. The last major crisis of world capitalism prior to the 2008 global financial collapse began in the late 1960s and hit hard in the early 1970s. The year 1968 was a turning point. That year saw the assassination of Martin Luther King Jr. in the United States in the midst of expanding Black and Chicano liberation movements; the counter-cultural and the anti-war movements; and an escalation of militant worker struggles. The Tlatelolco massacre of students took place in Mexico City that same year, at a time of great campesino, worker, and student upheavals across the country. The year 1968 also saw the Prague Spring, the uprising of students and workers in Paris, the height of the Cultural Revolution in China, the Tet Offensive in Vietnam (which marked the beginning of the first major defeat for U.S. imperialism), and the spread of anti-colonial and armed liberation movements throughout Africa and Latin America.

All this reflected a crisis of hegemony for the system – a crisis in its political and cultural domination. Then came the economic dimension. By 1973 the U.S. government had to abandon the gold standard; the recently formed Organization of Petroleum Exporting Countries (OPEC) imposed its oil embargo, which sent shock waves through the world economy; and stagflation (stagnation plus inflation) set in everywhere. This was, in a nutshell, a severe structural crisis of twentieth-century nation-state capitalism. By the early 1970s, a pre-revolutionary situation was percolating in many countries and regions. The popular classes were able to resist attempts by the dominant groups to shift the burden of the 1970s crises on to their shoulders.

As the crisis intensified, these dominant groups sought ways to liberate themselves from the social-democratic, redistributive "class compromise" arrangements of previous decades. Analytically speaking, capital sought to free itself of any reciprocal responsibility to labor in the capitalist system, and capitalist states sought to shed themselves of the social welfare systems that were established in preceding decades. Elites in the rich countries also sought ways to integrate emergent Third World elites into the system. These dominant groups launched the "neoliberal counter-revolution": an attempt to roll back the social welfare state, to resubordinate labor, and to reconstitute their hegemony at the global level through a newfound transnational mobility of capital and a transformation of the inter-state system.

The model of "savage" global capitalism that took hold in the late 20th century has involved a new capital–labor relation based on the deregulation, informalization, de-unionization, and flexibilization of labor. More and more workers have swelled the ranks of the "precariat": a proletariat existing in permanently precarious conditions. "Free-trade" agreements and neoliberal policies have played a key role in the subordination of labor worldwide and the creation of this flexible global labor market. The new model of global capitalism has also involved a renewed round of expansion of the system. The former socialist countries and the revolutionary states of the Third World were integrated into the world market in the late 20th century. But even more than this *extensive* expansion, the system has undergone *intensive* expansion. This involves the commodification of spheres of society previously outside of the logic of exchange value, such as social services, utilities, public lands, infrastructure, health, and education. These spheres then become sources of accumulation and the unloading of surplus capital. Let us put this into historic context.

The capitalist system has gone through successive waves of expansion and transformation since its bloody inception in 1492 with the conquest of the Americas. Each epoch has seen the reorganization of political and social institutions, and the rise of new class agents and technologies on the heels of major structural crises. These changes have resulted in new waves of outward expansion through wars of conquest, imperialism, and colonialism that bring more of humanity and of the planet into the orbit of capital. In the dialectical and historical-materialist approach, the distinct and varied social institutions, such as the educational system, are connected with one another, are grounded in political economy (that is, in the process of the production and reproduction of our material existence), and experience ongoing transformation in consort with the changing nature of the social order. Each epoch of world capitalism therefore has had implications for the major institutions that comprise society.

The mercantile era spanned the sixteenth, seventeenth, and early eighteenth centuries and saw the creation of a world market. This was followed by an epoch of classical competitive capitalism inaugurated with the French Revolution of 1789. This period brought in its wake the first industrial revolution, the definitive triumph of the bourgeoisie as a ruling class, and the consolidation of the nation-state and the inter-state system as the political form of the capitalist system. Competitive capitalism gave way to the rise of corporate capital, powerful national monopolies, and capitalist classes in the core capitalist countries. These countries organized themselves around protected national markets and engaged in a new round of imperialist expansion and inter-state competition over world markets, resources, and labor reserves. It took two world wars and many mass social struggles around the world for corporate capitalism to stabilize around a new "social structure of accumulation" (SSA): a pattern of accumulation involving a distinct and identifiable set of institutions, social norms, and political structures that facilitate a period of expanded accumulation.

But the Fordist–Keynesian SSA that took hold following the Second World War, with its mechanisms of redistribution, state intervention to regulate the market, and "class compromise," entered into a deep structural crisis in the 1970s. Emergent transnational capital responded to that crisis of the 1970s by "going global," giving way to the current epoch of global capitalism. One key distinctive feature of the current epoch is that the system has all but exhausted possibilities for *extensive* expansion, as the whole world has been brought into the orbit of capital. Globalization therefore involves an *intensive* expansion that is reaching depths not seen in previous epochs. The life-world itself, to use Habermas's phrase, becomes colonized by capital, and the educational system is one institution for this colonization.

Transnational capital, the transnational state, and commodification of education

Global capitalism involves a re-articulation of social power relations around the world. This new epoch is characterized by the rise of transnational capital and the integration of every country and region into a new globalized system of production, finances, and services. We have seen a sequence in the rise of the global economy. Production was the first to transnationalize, starting in the late 1970s; this shift was epitomized by the "global assembly line" and the spread of *maquiladoras* and *zonas francas* based on the super-exploitation of cheap, mostly young and female workers.

Next to transnationalize, in the 1990s and early 2000s, were national banking and financial systems. This followed the deregulation of banking and financial markets in most countries around the world and the creation of countless new "financial instruments" or tradable forms of finance. There is no longer such a thing as a national financial system. Given its fungible nature and its virtually complete digitalization, money moves almost frictionlessly through the financial circuits of the global economy and plays a key integrative function. Transnational finance capital has become the hegemonic fraction of capital on a world scale; it determines the circuits of capital and has subordinated productive capital to itself, not to mention the subordination of governments, political systems, social institutions, and households.

More recent is the transnationalization of services. By the second decade of the twenty-first century, the major thrust of "free-trade" negotiations, such as the Trade in Services Agreement, was aimed at removing remaining national regulation and public control of services, including finance, utilities, infrastructure, transportation, health, and education. Capitalist globalization has been a process of ongoing liberation of transnational capital from the nation-state and from popular and working-class constraints on its control, of the prerogative of accumulation over any social consideration, and of the progressive "commodification of everything."

But transnational capital is not faceless. A transnational capitalist class (TCC) has emerged as the manifest agent of global capitalism. National capitalist classes began to internationalize early in the twentieth century. As the process accelerated in the post-WWII period, especially following the 1970s crisis, capitals from core countries began to interpenetrate through numerous mechanisms that I and others have documented. These include through foreign direct and cross-investment, the transnational interlocking of boards of directors, transnational mergers and acquisitions, vast networks of outsourcing, subcontracting, joint ventures and alliances, and the establishment of tens of thousands of transnational corporate subsidiaries. Multinational corporations gave way to the giant global or transnational corporations that now drive the global economy. The TCC is grounded in emergent global circuits of accumulation rather than national circuits. The TCC has become the hegemonic fraction of the capitalist class on a global scale and at its apex is transnational finance capital. Power in most countries has gravitated away from local and national fractions of the elite, as well as from the popular classes, and toward transnationally oriented capitalist and elites.

Transnational fractions of the elite have vied for and in most countries taken state power, whether by elections or other means, and whether through the takeover of existing parties or the creation of entirely new political platforms, backed by powerful corporate business groups. As these transnationally oriented elites have captured national states, they have used the political control and cultural and ideological influence that accrues to material domination to push economic restructuring and capitalist globalization. In this way, they integrate their countries into the new global circuits of accumulation, as well as into the global legal and regulatory regime, such as the World Trade Organization (WTO), that is still under construction. These neoliberal states have opened up each national territory to transnational corporate plunder of resources, labor, and markets. Neoliberalism, as is well known, involves the deregulation and privatization of services, including educational systems.

As the TCC and its political and bureaucratic allies push for capitalist globalization, nation-states adopt corresponding neoliberal policies and sign "free-trade" agreements in consort with one another and with the supra- and transnational institutions that have designed and facilitated the global capitalist project (including the WTO, the International Monetary Fund (IMF), the World Bank, the European Union, the United Nations, and the Organization of Economic Cooperation and Development (OECD)). This increasingly dense network of nation-state institutions and trans- and supranational organizations comprise transnational state (TNS) apparatuses. The TNS promotes globalized circuits of accumulation and the power of transnational capital in each country. It is through TNS apparatuses that the TCC attempts to exercise its class power in each country and in the global system as a whole. Such TNS institutions as the World Bank and the IMF have been at the forefront of the neoliberal restructuring of educational systems, including the commodification of schooling and the privatization of higher education.

The changing labor needs of the global economy and the new precariat

In the classic study *Schooling in Capitalist America*, Bowles and Gintis showed how the internal organization of schools corresponded to the internal organization of the capitalist workforce in its structures, norms, and values. Their "correspondence theory" shows how the school system, with its disciplinary processes, hierarchal relations, and hidden curricula, prepared students for their futures in the capitalist economy. Schools, they showed, played a critical role in the capitalist class control of labor and in the reproduction of extant social inequalities.

Bowles and Gintis's essential point about the relationship between education, the capitalist economy, and society remains valid today. The factors that *have* changed are the nature of capitalism (specifically its globalization) and the changing labor needs of the global economy. Bowles and Gintis argued that there was a contradiction between the needs of *accumulation* and the needs of *social reproduction*. The capitalist economy needed a workforce that was highly trained, *intelligent*, and self-directed. The education required for this workforce also developed people's ability to think, and brought together millions of young people under conditions that could encourage struggles for social justice. Now, global capitalism needs a workforce with less autonomy and creative ability, and one subject to ever more intense mechanisms of social control in the face of a rising tide of superfluous labor and ever more widespread immiseration and insecurity. The hidden curriculum and the ideological content of mass education remain in place around the world, but the openly and directly repressive elements of education now play a heightened role.

Bowles and Gintis analyzed the development of education in the epochs of competitive and monopoly capitalism. The successive waves of the industrial revolution from the late eighteenth into the early twentieth century required a workforce with increasing knowledge and skills. Fordist–Keynesian capitalism needed a mass of semi-skilled and highly skilled workers, whether in the industrial heartlands of the world system or in the urban pockets of *import substitution industrialization* in the Third World. In addition, Third World elites promoting capitalist developmentalism sought to generate national educational systems that were often modeled on those of the core countries.

But as globalization has intensified, so too has the dual process of Taylorism and deskilling that was so strikingly analyzed by Harry Braverman in his classic and quite prescient study, *Labor and Monopoly Capital*. Meanwhile, several waves of the "scientific and technological revolution," especially computer and information technology, have made redundant much skilled and semi-skilled human labor. Jeremy Rivkin described this process, two decades after Braveman's study, in his popular book, *The End of Work*. Aronowitz and DiFazio discuss the same issue more recently in *The Jobless Future*. Just as the world's population is increasingly polarized between the 80 and the 20 per cent, so too work is ever more polarized. On the one hand there is the unskilled and low-skilled labor on the farms, in the factories, and in the office and service complexes of the global economy, as well as in the armed and security forces of the global police state. On the other hand are the highly skilled technical and knowledge workers. It is likely that the revolutions just getting underway in nanotechnology, bioengineering, 3D manufacturing, blockchain, autonomously driven vehicles, the Internet of Things, and robotic and machine intelligence – the revolutionary technologies of the immediate future, the so-called "fourth industrial revolution" – will only heighten this tendency toward bifurcation in the world's workforce.

To reiterate, then, global capital needs a mass of humanity that has basic numeracy and literacy skills and not much more, alongside high-tech educational training for highly skilled and knowledge workers. There are a handful of global elite universities that educate and groom the TCC, its organic intellectuals, and transnationally oriented managerial and technocratic elites. Examples include Harvard, Yale, Cambridge, Oxford, the Swiss Federal Institute of Technology, Tokyo University, the Indian Institute of Technology, and the *grandes écoles* in France. Elise Brezis estimates that the top fifty universities around the world recruit 33 per cent of transnational political elites and 47 per cent of transnational business elites. While most of these global elite universities are located in the United States, the network of elite universities now turns to new transnational student markets to recruit from around the world. Below the elite universities are higher education institutions intended to train people for a mercantile insertion into the upper rungs of the global labor market. Meanwhile, in the 1990s, just as the neoliberal onslaught was in full swing, TNS institutions began calling for universal primary education, alongside a shift from public to private secondary education and the privatization and commodification of higher education.

The World Bank has played the lead role in establishing the transnational elite's policy agenda in this regard. Its landmark 2003 report, *Achieving Universal Primary Education by 2015*, called for primary education to become universal by the year 2015, expanding on the call for such universal education contained in the United Nation's *Millennium Development Goals* promulgated with much fanfare in 2000 at the United Nations Millennium Summit and with the participation of so-called civil society representatives. The Millennium Development Goals put forth a set of eight targets to be achieved by 2015, among them:

- a reduction by half the proportion of people living in extreme poverty and who suffer from hunger;
- universal primary education;
- a reduction by two thirds the mortality rate among children under five and by three quarters of the maternal mortality rate;
- halt and reverse the incidence of major diseases;
- promote gender equality and the empowerment of women;

and so on. However, the prescription put forth to achieve these lofty goals was based on a more thoroughgoing privatization of health and educational systems; further freeing up the market from state regulations; greater trade liberalization and more structural adjustment; and the conversion of agricultural lands into private commercial property. In other words, the proposed solution was an intensification of the very capitalist development that had generated the social conditions to be eradicated.

The 2003 World Bank report made clear than an expansion of access and curricular and structural changes in education would be for the purpose of preparing workers for jobs in the global economy, and that educational reform would take place within a neoliberal policy framework. It argued that universal primary education when "combined with sound [read: neoliberal] macroeconomic policies" is essential to "globally competitive economies," to sustaining growth, and to increasing labor productivity. The report stressed that equitably distributing primary educational opportunity should not be confused with "the redistribution of other assets such as land or capital." It also specified that it was calling for public sector *financing* of primary schooling, but not necessarily *provision*. This is important because privatization often takes the form of governments creating markets for the corporate seizure of public education, and the provision of public subsidies for privately run schools such as charter schools.

At the same time as the World Bank and other TNS institutions have called for universal primary education in order to assure the provision of a labor force for global capitalism, they have pushed for the privatization of higher education. In its 1998 report, *Higher Education Financing Project*, the World Bank called for higher education programs to be privatized, deregulated, and "oriented to the market rather than public ownership or governmental planning and regulation." The report argued for substantial increases in university tuition fees; charging full fees for room and board; offering loans to students based on market interest rates, together with the subcontracting of private companies to collect student loan repayments; expanding "entrepreneurial training" at universities; programs to offer university research findings to corporate purchases; and a general increase in the number of private institutions with a progressive decrease in public education. The report's author stated in an addendum that

> "... much of what may look like the agenda of the neoliberal economist may also be more opportunistic than ideological. With taxes increasingly avoidable and otherwise difficult to collect and with competing public needs so compelling on all countries, an increasing reliance on tuition, fees and the unleashed entrepreneurship of the faculty may be the only alternative to a totally debilitating austerity."

This neoliberalization of higher education converts the university worldwide into the domain of the elite and that 20 per cent of humanity with the resources to finance their education and to train for taking commanding roles in global society. At the same time, it heightens the ideological role that education plays in inculcating dull minds, respect for authority, obedience, a craving for petty consumption and fantasy – that is, the banal culture of global capitalism and its dehumanizing values. Neoliberal restructuring, and, most importantly, privatization, opens up educational systems as a new space for accumulation and as a brain trust for transnational capital. The university and the educational system have been invaded by transnational capital in every sense, from converting education into a for-profit activity, to commissioning and appropriating research (often publicly funded) and generating a major new source of financial speculation through student loans.

Neoliberal restructuring has extended around the world what Slaughter and Leslie called "academic capitalism," or the development of functional linkages between higher education and corporate "knowledge capitalism." In the United States, where Slaughter and Leslie focused their research, the corporate takeover of higher education has involved the bifurcation of the professoriate into a small core of tenured professors and an army of precaritized or contract instructors. Adjunct faculty now teach over 70 per cent of all university courses in the United States. The switch from public funding of higher education to tuition-led funding has contributed to the student debt, which increased over 400 per cent from 2000 to 2013, when it reached $1.2 trillion. These mechanisms of debt bondage lock out would-be surplus labor from access to public higher education. Instead, the poorest are forced to turn to for-profit private "universities" that have proliferated since the turn of the century, with enrollment increasing 2017 per cent from 2000 to 2014 (compared to 25 per cent for public universities and for private non-profit institutions).

There is a double movement here. Capitalist globalization has involved a shift in the low-skilled and unskilled labor-intensive phases of global production circuits from the North to the South. At the same time, work in general has become bifurcated into deskilled and highly skilled jobs. Thus the neoliberal program of universal primary education and the privatization and commodification of secondary and higher education is reciprocal to changes in the global division of labor, as well as to the transformation in labor and the "end of work."

Global police state and ideological hegemony, on and off campus

The extreme inequalities of the global political economy cannot easily be contained through consensual mechanisms of social control. The great challenge the system faces is how to contain the actual and potential rebellion of the global working class and the surplus population. Relations of inequality and domination in global society include the increasing salience of new transnational class inequalities relative to the older forms of North–South inequality; a resurgence of racial and ethnic hierarchies; and a new worldwide class of immigrant workers denied the rights of citizenship and held in labor peonage. Frightening systems of mass social control and repression are spreading. The ruling groups have launched farcical wars on drugs, "gangs" (and youth more generally), "terrorism," and immigrants. These are wars of social control and dispossession being waged against the popular and working classes and the surplus labor population. These wars have engulfed social and political institutions, including educational systems. The TCC has taken up this challenge by imposing fear and obedience and assuring the social control of youth, in part by converting schools into centers for repressive discipline and ruthless punishment. The role of schooling in social control is an old theme, but the coupling of the educational system with new systems of mass social control and surveillance is reaching depths hitherto unseen.

The U.S. press is full of stories that stretch the imagination on the militarization of public schools, the criminalization of students, and extreme disciplinary punishment as the school-to-prison pipeline becomes ever more institutionalized. Class relations in the United States have historically been highly racialized, and the racialized nature of this criminalization and punishment cannot be over-emphasized. In many states, public school students are now thrown into jail for tardiness and absences. According to a complaint filed with the U.S. Department of Justice in June 2013, students in Texas have been taken out of school in handcuffs, held in jail for days at a time, and fined more than $1,000 for missing more than ten days of school. According to the complaint, school grounds are run like a police state, with guards rounding up students during "tardy sweeps," suspending them, and then marking their absences as unexcused even when students have legitimate reasons for absence, such as family emergency or illness. The Pentagon has supplied schools throughout the United States with military-grade weapons and vehicles, and even with grenade launchers. Schools have spied on students in their home by supplying laptop computers with webcams that are activated by remote control. The surveillance state has invaded the public school system with CCTV cameras, security checkpoints, full time armed guards, and military recruiters – especially in poor, working-class, and racially oppressed communities.

This militarization of schools brings about a convergence of schools in the school systems that serve working-class and racially oppressed communities with the criminal justice system – to such an extent that the two systems appear as nothing less than a single institutional continuum. Gilmore has shown how mass incarceration has both provided the state with a means of caging surplus labor, disproportionately from racially oppressed communities, and provided capital with a means of unloading surplus and sustaining accumulation. The regime of repression and punishment in the public school system is the juvenile corollary to mass incarceration. As broad swaths of the working class become surplus labor, schools in marginalized communities "prepare" students for prison and "social death" rather than for a life of labor.

Meanwhile, high-stakes standardized testing – itself a lucrative source of corporate accumulation – aims to impose a dull uniformity on curricula. It reduces learning to rote memorization, routine, punctuality, and obedience in regimented classrooms. Meanwhile, non-conforming teachers are disciplined and teachers' unions are attacked. Handwritten essays are not evaluated by experienced educators, but by temp workers hired seasonally at low wages and assigned to grade up to forty essays an hour. One for-profit test-scoring company, Pearson, operates 21 scoring centers around the United States, hiring 14,500 temp scorers during the scoring season. Results are then used to defund and close "non-performing" schools. Teachers received pre-packaged lesson plans that are scripted to prepare for the tests. High-stakes testing leads to the segregation of learning and the bifurcation of schools into those catering to the well-off and those serving the working class and surplus labor that closely mirrors the new spatial apartheid in urban centers. Punitive standardized testing and the spread of charter schools, admission to which is determined by test performance, facilitates co-optation of promising (and obedient) students from the working-class and racially/ethnically oppressed communities into the would-be ranks of the 20 per cent as technocratic and knowledge workers.

The hidden curriculum of ideological hegemony, socialization into hierarchy and conformity, and the suppression of critical thinking plays a heightened role in global capitalism. "The ideas of the ruling class are in every epoch the ruling ideas," Marx famously observed in *The German Ideology*. "The class that is the ruling material force of society, is at the same time its ruling intellectual force," he went on. "The class that has the means of material production at its disposal has control at the same time over the means of mental production, so that thereby, generally speaking, the ideas of those who lack the means of mental production are subject to it. The ruling ideas are nothing more than the ideal expression of the dominant material relationships, the dominant material relationships grasped as ideas."

The "dominant material relationships" of global capitalism are expressed in the ideologies of neoliberalism, multiculturalism, individualism, martial masculinity, militarism, and as well in postmodern pessimism. As Argentine scholar Atilio Boron observes in his excellent study on the role of the World Bank and of neoliberalization of education in undermining critical thought:

> "... It is extremely difficult and costly to escape the formidable intellectual vice of the nefarious combination of neoclassical economics and postmodernism, the result of which has been a deeply conservative and conformist mode of thought imbued with a broad repertoire of subtle mechanisms of ideological control which cut at the very roots the growth of critical thought in the university, not to mention at the level of the mass media and public space in general)."

Boron goes on to note that until the mid-twentieth century, public universities predominated in Latin America, and indeed there were almost no private universities of significance. But by 2008, 60 per cent of all universities in Latin America were private, accounting for some 40 per cent of all student enrollments. In some countries, such as Brazil, Chile, and Colombia, private universities were coming to eclipse entirely the public university. At the same time, Boron reports, there has been a deleterious deterioration in the quality of education at the public universities, together with defunding, rising student fees, a decline in instructor earnings, and a shift to part-time and contract instructors. Education increased slightly from 1985 to 2005 as a percentage of gross national product (GNP) in most Latin American countries, while during this same time, spending on higher education declined significantly in almost every country, and in some cases dropped precipitously.

As the neoliberal commodification of higher education proceeds, "the classic ideal that conceived of education as a process for the cultivation and integral development of the human spirit has been abandoned" and replaced by a crude "mercantile and utilitarian conception of education as training in order to learn the skills that the market demands and to assure the 'employability' of the student." Higher education has become a "service." One of the consequences of the neoliberal takeover of higher education has been, in Boron's words, "the generalized acceptance now enjoyed by the previously bizarre idea that universities should be considered as profitable institutions that generate income generated by the 'sale of their services.'"

Boron calls for "critical and radical thought" *contra* neoliberal ideology diffused through the educational and mass media systems of global capitalism. His call, although aimed at Latin America, is equally appropriate for global society as a whole:

"An observer who came down from Mars might ask, 'why does Latin America need radical thought?' The answer: for a very simple reason; because the situation in Latin America is radically unjust, so absolutely unjust and so much more unjust with each passing year, that if we want to make a contribution to the social life of our countries, to the wellbeing of our peoples, we have no other alternative but to critically rethink our society, to explore 'other possible worlds' that allow us to move beyond the crisis and to communicate with the mass of people who make history in a plain, simple, and understandable language."

Conclusion: Revitalizing a philosophy of praxis

A global rebellion against the rule of the TCC has spread since the financial collapse of 2008. Wherever one looks around the world, there is an escalation of popular and grassroots social justice struggles and a rise of new cultures of resistance. At the same time, the crisis has produced a rapid political polarization between a resurgent left and a neo-fascist right. The far right is often driven by ethnic nationalisms and the manipulation of fear and insecurity experienced by downwardly mobile and precaritized working-class communities. In recent years, these communities have been targeted for recruitment to neo-fascist projects by far-right forces in a number of countries, including in the United States, where these forces mobilized behind the Trump candidacy in the 2016 elections and then provided a critical base of support for the Trump presidency. How these struggles play out will depend, in part, on how effectively popular forces from below manage to construct a counter-hegemony to that of the transnational ruling bloc. The prospects for such a counter-hegemony depend on how the crisis is understood and interpreted by masses of people. This, in turn, depends on a *systemic* critique of global capitalism and on organic intellectuals of the popular classes – in the Gramscian sense, as intellectuals who attach themselves to and serve the emancipatory struggles of the popular classes – committed to putting forth such a critique.

Alongside the economic restructuring of capitalist globalization since the 1980s, organic intellectuals of the emerging TCC responded at the cultural level to the popular and revolutionary uprisings of the 1960s and the 1970s with a strategy of "diversity" and "multiculturalism" to reconstruct ideological hegemony. The strategy aimed to neuter through co-optation the demands for social justice and anti-capitalist transformation. Dominant groups would now welcome representation in the institutions of capital and power but would suppress, violently if necessary, struggles to overthrow capital or simply curb its prerogatives. Some among the historically oppressed groups gained representation in the institutions of power; others aspired to do so.

They condemned oppression but banished *exploitation* from the popular vocabulary.

In Latin America, the dominant groups violently repressed the "Indio Insurreccionista" (the insurrectionary Indian) who demanded control over land and resources, and encouraged the "Indio Permitido" who would be allowed to seek cultural pluralism and political representation but was not to question the capitalist social order and its structure of property and class power. On U.S. university campuses, cultural and identity politics took over. Dominant groups now praised – even championed – opposition to racism as personal injury and "micro-aggressions" that eclipsed any critique of the macro-aggressions of capitalism and the link between racial oppression and class exploitation – what Aviva Chomsky terms "the politics of the left-wing of neoliberalism." She points out that university administrators are attempting now to absorb into "the market-oriented system of higher education" a new upsurge of student activism in the United States that has placed climate change, inequality, immigrant rights, and opposition to mass incarceration at the forefront of campus struggles. Yet the term "neoliberalism" has become a stand-in for "capitalism." Critique of neoliberalism as a set of policies (liberalization, privatization, deregulation, etc.) and an accompanying ideology that has facilitated capitalist globalization cannot substitute critique of global capitalism.

A critical part of the construction of any counter-hegemonic project will take place in schools and university campuses around the world. Throughout the Americas, my own focal point of scholar-activism, teachers have led the struggle against neoliberal educational reform, the privatization of education, the defunding and closure of schools, the de-unionization of the profession, and state repression of students. They have stood alongside the remarkable student mobilizations in Mexico, Chile, Brazil, the United States, and elsewhere. There is a need to infuse student struggles and workers' uprisings with radical global political economy theory and analysis that can contribute to the practices of global social justice and emancipatory struggles – that is, to what Antonio Gramsci called a *philosophy of praxis*.

Capital has an International and it is going fascist

Time for an International of the global popular classes

First published in *Globalizations*, 2019

The renowned Egyptian-born scholar and global South activist Samir Amin put out a call just before his death in 2018 for "workers and peoples" to establish a "fifth international". His call sparked broad discussion on the international left, and it could not have been timelier. If we are to face the onslaught of the neo-fascist right, the left worldwide must urgently renovate a revolutionary project and a plan for re-founding the state. It must do so across borders, under an umbrella organization or platform that puts forth a minimum program around which popular and working-class forces can unite, and that establishes mechanisms for transnational struggle. While I concur with much of Amin's call, I also have some significant differences as well as specifications with respect to the call that I will attempt to explicate below.

Global capitalism is facing a spiraling crisis of hegemony that appears to be approaching a general crisis of capitalist rule. In the face of this crisis, there has been a sharp polarization in global society between, on the one hand, an insurgent left and popular forces, and, on the other, an insurgent far right with openly fascist tendencies at its fringe. Yet the far right has been more effective than the left in the past few years at mobilizing disaffected populations around the world, and has made significant political and institutional inroads. Given the magnitude of the means of violence worldwide and the threat of ecological holocaust, Rosa Luxemburg's dire warning at the start of WWI that we face "socialism or barbarism" is as relevant today, or even more so, than when she issued it. If left, popular, and working-class forces are to regain the initiative and beat back barbarism, they need a transnational umbrella organization with a minimum program against global capitalism around which they can coordinate national and regional struggles and *transnationalize* the fightback.

The international of capital and the specter of twenty-first-century fascism

The theme of transnational struggles from below has been discussed at great length for several decades now. Capital has achieved a newfound transnational mobility, yet labor remains territorially bound by the nation-state. In the wake of the structural crisis of the 1970s, emergent transnational capital went global as a strategy to reconstitute its social power by breaking free of nation-state constraints to accumulation, to do away with Fordist–Keynesian redistributive arrangements, and to beat back the tide of revolution in the Third World.

As the rate of profit declined in the 1970s, the corporate class and its agents identified state regulation, and the mass struggles and demands of popular and working classes, as fetters to its freedom to make profits and accumulate wealth. As an emergent transnational capitalist class (TCC) congealed, it put in place a new transnational corporate order and went on the offensive in its class warfare against working and popular classes. Globalization enhanced the structural power of transnational capital over states and popular classes worldwide. Behind this alleged "loss of state sovereignty," capitalist globalization changed the correlation of class forces worldwide in favor of the TCC. Transnational capital has been able to exercise a newfound structural power over states and territorially bound working classes, which has undermined the ability of states to capture and redistribute surpluses, and with it, the logic and basis for social democratic projects. This is the backdrop to what Amin identifies as the political neutering of traditional unions and left-wing parties and their organizations.

We should be clear that, despite nationalist and populist rhetoric, the forces of twenty-first-century fascism do not constitute a departure from global capitalism but, to the contrary, their program advances the interests of transnational capital in the face of overaccumulation and stagnation in the global economy. The fight against fascism is necessarily a fight against the TCC. The core of twenty-first-century fascism is the triangulation of transnational capital with reactionary and repressive political power in the state, and neo-fascist forces in civil society. Emergent twenty-first-century fascist projects are a response to the crisis. Escalating inequalities, and the inability of global capitalism to assure the survival of billions of people, have thrown states into crises of legitimacy, and now push the system toward more openly repressive means of social control and domination that exacerbate political and social conflict and international tensions. Neo-fascist projects are a contradictory attempt to re-found state legitimacy under the destabilizing conditions of capitalist globalization.

Each neo-fascist project springs from particular national histories and circumstances, and is therefore distinct. However, Trumpism in the United States, Bolsonarism in Brazil, Milei in Argentina, the extreme-right Netanyahu regime in Israel, neo-fascist and far-right nationalist parties in Europe, Modi's Hindu fundamentalist state in India, and to varying degrees other far-right movements around the world, all represent the extension of capitalist globalization by other means, namely by an expanding global police state and a neo-fascist mobilization. They seek to create a new balance of political forces in the face of the breakdown of the short-lived historic global capitalist bloc. What is emerging is an International of twenty-first century fascism. Far-right and neo-fascist groups around the world, for instance, celebrated the October 2018 electoral victory of Brazilian fascist Jair Bolsonaro. Former Trump adviser and neo-fascist organizer Steven Bannon served as an adviser to the Bolsonaro campaign. Meanwhile, Italy's extreme-right interior minister Matteo Salvini declared in an exuberant tweet (that was shared by U.S. neo-Nazi leader Richard Spencer) that "even in Brazil, the citizens have sent the left packing." *The Guardian* of London warned in its headline coverage that "Trump joy over Bolsonaro suggests new rightwing axis in Americas and beyond." While Bolsonaro himself was voted out of power in 2022 and Brazil swung again to the left of center under a new Workers Party government, political polarization continued throughout South America, with the neo-fascist Javier Milei elected in Argentina in 2023.

Beyond such political agents of a twenty-first century fascism as Bannon, Salvini, Trump, or Modi, the TCC had banked (literally) on Bolsonaro in 2018 and was delighted with his victory. As in the

United States under Trump, Bolsonaro proposed the wholesale privatization and deregulation of the economy, opening up the amazon to lumber, mining, and transnational agribusiness interests. He introduced regressive taxation and general austerity, alongside mass repression and criminalization of social movements and vulnerable communities that opposed this program. As one journalist noted at the time of Bolsonaro's electoral victory, the "world's capitalists are salivating over the new investment opportunities" that he promised. Capital markets and Brazilian funds spiked on the world's stock exchanges the day after his electoral victory. Here we see the "wages of fascism" for a global capitalism in crisis.

A new international and a united front against twenty-first century fascism

The right has drawn on the well-known nationalist, populist, xenophobic, and racist repertoire to channel rising anxieties and transform mass anti-systemic sentiment into support for its neo-fascist program. We should be clear, however, that it has been the inability of the left to confront global capitalism and to put forth a clear leftist alternative that has paved the way for the neo-fascist right. The case of Brazil is particularly indicative. During its 14 years in power, the Workers Party courted national and transnational capital, overseeing a dramatic expansion of capitalist globalization in the country. It demobilized the mass movements that had brought it to power and absorbed its leaders into the state. Its renowned social welfare programs depended entirely on mild redistribution during the boom period of high prices for the country's commodities exports. Once the prices collapsed in 2014 and the economy tanked, the far right, with the backing of the TCC in Brazil and abroad, moved on the offensive. The Workers Party program did not deviate substantially from this when it returned to power in 2022.

The lessons from Brazil, Latin America, the United States, and elsewhere are clear. When faced with the inability of moderate reform to stabilize capitalism or neo-fascism, the political and economic elite will embrace the latter. And when a program of mild reform alongside capitalist globalization fails to resolve the plight of masses of people, some of these masses will embrace the fascist alternative. This is why the new International that Amin calls for must stake out a clear position in frontal attack against global capitalism.

These lessons have been particularly painful in Latin America, where the Pink Tide (left turn) starting in the new century raised great hopes and expectations. As has now been discussed at some length by many, myself included, the left in state power (with the partial exception of Venezuela and, to a lesser extent, Bolivia) did not undertake structural transformations; it did not challenge the prevailing property relations and class structure. Social assistance programs depended on the whims of the global market controlled by the TCC. When the price of the region's commodities exports collapsed, starting in 2011, the left lost the very basis for its mildly reformist project.

The popular masses were clamoring for more substantial transformations. But under the pretext of attracting transnational corporate investment to bring about development, the demands from below for deeper transformation were often suppressed. Social movements were demobilized, their leaders absorbed by the institutional left in government and the capitalist state, and their mass bases subordinated to the left parties' electoralism. There is now an evident disjuncture throughout Latin America between mass social movements that are at this time resurgent, and the institutional and party left that is losing power and influence by the day and that, even when it wins elections, does not challenge the rule of capital but rather re-legitimizes it. This disjuncture must be closed and the relationship between political organizations and social movements needs to be clarified as part of the work of a new International.

Here is where we need a new International that puts forth a unified minimal program coordinated across borders and across regions. The World Social Forum (WSF) explicitly rejected a political program and thus contributed to the separation of left political parties from mass social movements. For a fightback to be successful, we need to build a united front against fascism and a program around which such a united front can be organized. Infighting within the ruling groups is escalating as the historic global capitalist bloc – constructed in the heyday of neoliberalism from the 1990s until the financial collapse of 2008 – now unravels. (More broadly, the whole post-WWII international system is collapsing, and very rapidly, but that is a discussion to take up elsewhere.) Such infighting may present opportunities for the popular classes to build broad political alliances in the struggle against fascism.

Historically, such fronts have subordinated the left to the reform-oriented and "democratic" bourgeoisie. This time around, in my view, any strategy of broad anti-fascist alliances must foreground a clear and sharp analysis of global capitalism and its crisis, and strive for popular and working-class forces to exercise their hegemony over such alliances. For this, we need an International with a program. Amin notes that such an International would require several years' development before producing any tangible results. We should not be under any illusions that a new International as called for by Amin will be free of conflict. All to the contrary, we will push forward in the midst of sharp debate among many different and even antagonistic positions. In the real course of history, this is inevitable.

The challenge of Amin's call for an International of workers and peoples

But the construction of programs must also involve debate over the analysis of global capitalism that is at once political and theoretical. It is here that I have significant disagreements with Amin. He notes, correctly, in my view, the centralization of power and the extreme concentration of capital worldwide. However, I disagree with his confused insistence on a territorial (rather than a class/social) concentration of that capital and power, and with his insistence on evolving a "triad" (United States, Europe, Japan) framework that ignores the worldwide transnationalization of capital and the rise of powerful contingents of the TCC in the former Third World.

Amin's nation-state/triad framework is his blind spot. It is anecdotally illustrative that the 2018 report on the world's rich, issued by the Swiss bank UBS, notes that most of the world's billionaires are in the United States, but the number of ultra-wealthy people is growing fastest throughout Asia. In China, which now accounts for one in five of the world's billionaires, two new billionaires are minted every week. China's economic role in Africa, Asia, and Latin America now appears structurally the same as the traditional triad countries. Brazilian, Mexican, Indian, Saudi, Egyptian, and other capitalists who belong to the TCC now also invest worldwide in these same structures, including extensive investment *in* the triad countries. Another report by *Forbes* noted that wealth is growing faster among the super-rich in the former Third World than elsewhere. "Between 2012 and 2017, Bangladesh saw its ultra-rich club grow by 17.3%," it noted. "Over the same time period, growth in China was 13.4% while in Vietnam it was 12.7%. Kenya and India were among the other nations recording double-digit growth of 11.7 and 10.7% respectively. The U.S. came tenth overall for the population growth of UHNWI [ultra-high net worth individuals] at 8.1% from 2012 to 2017." Amin is simply wrong when he asserts that "the oligarchs of the triad are the only ones that count."

Amin's persistent nation-state/inter-state framework of analysis of world political dynamics ignores both the "Thirdworldization" of significant sectors of the First-World working classes, and the rise of TCC contingents in the former Third World that are now globally active and part of the global investor class. It is in fact the downward mobility and destabilization of working classes in the former First World – the destruction of the old labor aristocracies – that provides the recruiting grounds for twenty-first century fascism *but also* establishes fertile new opportunities for transnational North–South solidarities (yet another reason why Amin's call for a new International is so urgent).

These are not merely analytical or theoretical differences. They have political implications insofar as we must banish any lingering illusions about a "progressive" or "nationalist" bourgeoisie in the former Third World with which one could ally against global capital. There may have been one in the bygone era of colonialism and the heyday of national liberation struggles in the twentieth century, but the interests of the leading contingents of capital and their political representatives in the former Third World now lie in the defense and consolidation of global capitalism. The "recolonization" of the world by what Amin refers to as the "collective imperialism" of the triad countries is in actuality a recolonization by the TCC, not by some nation-states of other nation-states – notwithstanding that the most powerful contingents of the TCC are still located in the old triad countries and now in China as well.

The worldwide struggle from below of a new International – which *must* be simultaneously national *and* transnational – must identify and prioritize the class antagonisms within and across countries and regions over core-periphery or global North–South contradictions, *even though* these latter contradictions are still very much relevant, if increasingly secondary. The irony is that Amin's "triad against the global South" framework of analysis is in direct contradiction with his entirely correct assertion that "the possibility of substantial progressive reforms of capitalism in its current stage is only an illusion."

Of course, the First, Second, Third, and Fourth Internationals were all international umbrella organizations for socialist political parties, whereas the WSF prohibited political parties from participating. I fully concur with Amin that we need to "establish a new Organization and not just a 'movement'" or a "discussion forum." At this time, in my view, it is necessary for a new International to incorporate both social movements and left political organizations and parties. This is to say that a new International would be quite distinct from the first four and also from the WSF, which was an International of social movements only. Commitment to a "minimum program" and to joining forces with political parties around such a program may be tough for social movements to swallow. It is absolutely true that the vanguardist model of revolution in the twentieth century involved control of social movements from below by political parties that sought to snuff out their autonomy, and moreover, that some left political organizations in and out of the state in the new century continue to seek such control over social movements from below. (As an aside – the vanguardist model was less due to Lenin's approach than to a fetishization of that approach.)

Clearly, a new International must put forth a model of revolutionary struggle in which social movements from below exercise complete autonomy from political parties, and from states that may be captured by such parties. If the left attempts to control or place brakes on mass mobilization and on autonomous social movements from below, if it suppresses the demands of the popular masses in the name of "governance" or electoral strategies, it will be betraying what it means to be left. It is only such mobilization from below that can impose a counterweight to the control that transnational capital and the global market exercise from above over capitalist states around the world.

Finally, any new International will have to deal with the matter of elections and of the capitalist state. We have learned that subordinating the popular agenda to winning elections will only set us up for defeat, even if we must participate in electoral processes when possible and expedient. But we must also learn from the experiences of Syriza in Greece and the Pink Tide governments in Latin America, as well as social democratic governments that came to office around the world in the late twentieth century. Once a left force wins government office (which is *not* the same as state power; state power is imposed structurally by transnational capital), it is tasked with administering the capitalist state and its crisis, and is pushed into defending that state and its dependence on transnational capital for its reproduction. This places it at odds with the same popular classes and social movements that brought it to power.

There is no ready solution to these dilemmas. But certainly, a new International of workers and peoples that entails "an actual organization with statutes and a renovated socialist project" is integral to a solution. Amin is right that "we are now in the phase of the 'autumn of capitalism' without this being strengthened by the emergence of 'the people's spring' and a socialist perspective."

Passive revolution and the movement against mass incarceration

From prison abolition to redemption script

First published in *Social Justice*, 2020

The movement that has come to be known as "prison abolition" has by now become a centerpiece of the left and progressive agenda in the United States, and increasingly around the world. Mass incarceration is spreading very rapidly from the United States to Latin America, Europe, Asia, and elsewhere. In 2023, the Salvadoran government inaugurated its draconian mega-prison, the "Center for the Confinement of Terrorism." It is, if we do not count the occupied Palestinian territories as one giant mega-prison, the largest in the world, with a capacity for forty thousand prisoners. Not to be outdone, China, Turkey, the Philippines, Thailand, and India, among other countries, have opened or are planning to open such mega-prisons of their own. The Penal Reform International program observed in its 2023 report, *Global Prison Trends 2023*, that there were in that year more people worldwide in prison than ever before (11.5 million) and that people locked up everywhere face conditions of extreme overcrowding, are subjects for the application of radical new social control technologies, suffer extraordinarily high death rates, lack access to legal aid and to adequate medical care, and face alarming escalation of prison violence.

Yet generally missing from official reports, journalistic headlines, and the prison abolition movement itself, is a class analysis of the relationship of mass incarceration to global capitalism and its crisis, including the exponential expansion of the surplus population worldwide and the fact that the vast majority of those incarcerated come from the lowest rungs of the global proletariat. This is not coincidental. The ruling groups themselves have a newfound interest in prison reform and have apparently set the parameters for public discussion on mass incarceration. There is a contradictory movement here. On the one hand, capitalist states must radically expand incarceration in order to contain surplus humanity. On the other hand, the ruling groups themselves have embraced the discourse of abolition. Let us here focus on the case of prison abolition in the United States, which still locks up the largest number of people of any country, because it offers an exemplary case study in the dynamics of hegemony and co-optation

The passage in 2019 of a United States prison reform bill (the First Step Act) was indicative of the newfound interest in prison reform among the dominant groups. The bill's various provisions included granting judges more discretion when sentencing drug offenders; reducing the sentence for some drug offenders with three convictions (or "three strikes", which stipulated that after any three criminal convictions, not matter what they are, one is automatically sentenced to life imprisonment) from life to 25 years; and boosting prison rehabilitation efforts, including educational and training programs that allowed prisoners to "earn credit." While Democrats and Republicans alike cheered the bill as a "breakthrough," particularly revealing was its endorsement by conservative and far-right groups, ranging from the Cato Institute to Americans for Prosperity (an organization backed by the Koch brothers). Even the Fraternal Order of Police and the union representing federal prison guards backed the bill. What accounted for this rather abrupt change of heart among the dominant groups?

The radical critique of mass incarceration and the movement for prison abolition have been around for half a century, if not longer. But the movement gained steam in the early twenty-first century, linking the call for abolition to a critique of global capitalism and empire, as Angela Davis, among others, has discussed. In her bestseller *Golden Gulag*, U.S. prison-abolitionist scholar Ruth Wilson Gilmore delivered a devastating critique of the relationship between crisis in capital accumulation and the expansion of the prison-industrial complex. However, it was with the publication in 2012 of Michelle Alexander's *The New Jim Crow: Mass Incarceration in the Age of Color Blindness*, that the mainstream took notice and began to embrace the movement against mass incarceration. Yet that embrace has been icy. Far from helping to do away with the causes and consequences of mass incarceration, it has all the makings of an attempt at what the Italian communist Antonio Gramsci referred to as *passive revolution* – that is, an attempt from above to bring about mild reform in order to undercut movements from below for more radical change.

The irony here should not be lost. The organizations and political agents of the corporate elite that have now embraced reform are the same ones that championed capitalist globalization and one of its byproducts, mass incarceration. The Cato Institute, for instance – founded in 1977 to promote the emerging neoliberal agenda of the corporate state, "free markets," and globalization – has done as much as any group among the power elite to push the very conditions of capitalist restructuring and class warfare. This push from above in the United States and worldwide over the past four decades has resulted in an exponential expansion of the ranks of surplus humanity – disproportionately drawn from racially oppressed populations – and the concomitant systems of mass social control and repression that in the first place produced mass incarceration.

Yet in recent years, the Institute has adopted prison reform as one of its major foci. The Cato Institute is joined in this newfound concern for over-incarceration and criminal justice reform by what appears to be the entire assortment of liberal and conservative corporate-funded think tanks and foundations in the United States. These include The Heritage Foundation, the Koch brothers, and the Ford, MacArthur, Kellogg, Rockefeller, Mellon, Soros, and Carnegie foundations. These foundations alone funded the Art for Justice Fund in 2017 to the tune of $100 million, to dole out grants in strategic doses to criminal justice reform groups.

As politicians, foundations, and the corporate media have taken up the matter of mass incarceration, the focus in the public agenda has shifted away from radical critique of mass incarceration and a push for abolition to mere reform, and away from the injustices of a brutal neoliberal global capitalism (which has generated the conditions leading to mass incarceration) to a redemption script. The theme of co-optation by capitalist philanthropy was first raised by Marx and Engels, who wrote in *The Communist Manifesto* that a sector of the capitalist class is "desirous of redressing social grievances in order to secure the continued existence" of their rule. More recently, in 2007, the collective INCITE! Women of Color Against Violence published their groundbreaking anthology, *The Revolution Will Not Be Funded: Beyond the Non-Profit Industrial Complex*. They described this complex as "a set of symbiotic relationships that link political and financial technologies of state and owning class control with surveillance over public political ideology, including and especially emergent progressive and leftist social movements."

In his remarkable study, *Under the Mask of Philanthropy*, Michael Barker shows how the politics of capitalist philanthropy is aimed at deflecting challenges to the system:

> "Reform or revolution? This is a question that is central to effective progressive social change. From many people's point of view there is little doubt that capitalism must be eradicated, so the only question that remains is "How might this revolutionary process proceed?" Revolutionary action does not negate reform, as radical reforms are a critical part of any socialist praxis of change. On the other hand, liberal reforms without revolutionary direction are unlikely to build the momentum that will be necessary to oust capitalism. Thus understanding how leading activists and intellectuals who were formerly committed to revolutionary social change give up on such principles and dedicate their lives to moderating capitalist oppression is critical for social and political movements seeking to resist such challenges."

The radical critique of mass incarceration that has gained traction in recent years has correctly linked it to capitalism, the mass repression of oppressed communities, and a ruthless prison-industrial complex bent on turning mass social control into multiple sources of accumulation. The danger here is that this critique will become eclipsed by the rise of the redemption script. In this script, the foundations and institutes of the corporate order fund researchers and activists to focus on the redemption of those incarcerated, in place of a radical critique of the prison-industrial complex. These ostensibly private institutions of the ruling class have set about to fund organizations, grassroots campaigns, and progressive groups that have taken up the struggle against mass incarceration. As the headline in one article by the industry publication, *Inside Philanthropy*, proclaimed: "Redemption: An Accelerator Puts Former Inmates in the Driver's Seat." The redemption script is all about helping those incarcerated and released to absorb capitalist ideology and integrate into the capitalist labor market as compliant workers and "social entrepreneurs":

> "With funders like the Ford Foundation, the Public Welfare Foundation and others footing the bill, a range of nonprofit and community groups have been helping the formerly incarcerated successfully reenter society. Techniques like job training, education (including by bringing college into prisons), and even "pay for success" programs have paid off. According to Tulaine Montgomery, who leads New Profit's Unlocked Futures program, job creation and economic opportunity are the surest ways to make those second chances stick.....[This] new initiative, Unlocked Futures, is an incubator that supports, in part, formerly incarcerated social entrepreneurs who've turned their lives around and want to give back. "This program is a rebuke to the narrative that 'these people' can't be viable business leaders," Montgomery told me. Unlocked Futures' first cohort includes eight entrepreneurs operating both nonprofit and for-profit ventures. They're all united by a "double bottom line"— succeeding in their own spheres and working to end mass incarceration. They get $50,000 each, plus individualized training, coaching and workshops over the course of 16 months."

Abolition, redemption, hegemony, and passive revolution

The Italian communist Antonio Gramsci developed the concept of passive revolution to refer to efforts by dominant groups to bring about mild change from above in order to defuse mobilization from below for more far-reaching transformation. Integral to passive revolution is the co-optation of leadership from below and the integration of that leadership into the dominant project. Gramsci also referred to this process as *transformismo*, in which rule by the dominant groups is dependent on the ongoing absorption of intellectual, political, and cultural leaders of the subordinate majority into the ruling bloc, and the resulting decapitation and disorganization of resistance from below. Passive revolution comes into play at times when the system faces an impending crisis of hegemony. Whenever the hegemony of the bourgeoisie begins to disintegrate and a period of organic crisis develops, the process of reform or reorganization that is needed to re-establish its hegemony will to some extent have these characteristics of passive revolution.

Gramsci developed the general concept of hegemony to refer to the attainment by ruling groups of stable forms of rule based on "consensual" domination of subordinate groups. Gramsci's notion of hegemony posits distinct forms, or relations of domination. In brief, these are *coercive domination* and *consensual domination*. Hegemony is a relationship between classes or groups in which one class or group exercises leadership over other classes and groups by gaining their active consent. Hegemony is thus rule by consent, or the cultural and intellectual leadership achieved by a particular class, class fraction, strata, or social group, as part of a larger project of class rule or domination. All social order is maintained through a combination of consensual and coercive dimensions; in Gramsci's words, hegemony is "consensus protected by the armor of coercion." For Gramsci, then, the state is not all repression; it plays an "educative role," seeking consent through intellectuals and activists brought into the state's programs through political, professional, and syndical associations that are funded and organized by the private associations of capital and the ruling class.

In the wake of worldwide rebellions in the 1960s, and the crisis of world capitalism of the 1970s, emerging transnational elites launched capitalist globalization as a project to break resistance worldwide, regenerate global capital accumulation, and reconstitute the hegemony it had lost. These emerging transnational elites had carried out a passive revolution involving the reorganization of the world political economy and social relations, while neutralizing the resistance of the subordinate majority. They did this through a *combination* of consensual incorporation (co-optation) of leading strata of activists and organic intellectuals from below – often through "diversity" and "multicultural" agendas and the identitarian politics of "inclusion" – *and* the development of new systems of mass social control and repression. Capitalist globalization has effected an unprecedented expansion of the ranks of surplus labor that, in the United States, has been drawn disproportionately from racially oppressed communities – although as capitalist crisis and restructuring deepens, white proletarians are also experiencing precaritization and are swelling the ranks of surplus labor. That came to constitute the raw human refuse in need of mass caging, alongside other forms of social control carried out by an expanding global police state.

But in recent years, global capitalism is again facing a crisis of hegemony that has involved renewed challenge to the system by mass movements from below. These include the movement critiquing the prison-industrial complex, linking it to capitalism, and calling for its abolition. For passive revolution to succeed in stabilizing ruling class hegemony, the mild reform from above must also involve the diffusion of the ideological and programmatic content of reform and have it achieve hegemony over calls for more radical change. Hence legal reforms such as the First Step Act, and others undoubtedly to come, must also involve the diffusion of the redemption script so that it displaces abolition and the radical critique of the prison-industrial complex as the hegemonic narrative.

Abolition activist Dylan Rodriguez notes in his contribution to the activist book, *Abolition Now! Ten Years of Strategy and Struggle Against the Prison Industrial Complex*:

"Avowedly progressive, radical, leftist, and even some misnamed "revolutionary" groups find it opportune to assimilate into this state-sanctioned organizational paradigm, as it simultaneously allows them to establish a relatively stable financial and operational infrastructure while avoiding the transience, messiness, and possible legal complication of working under decentralized, informal, or even "underground" auspices. Thus, the aforementioned authors [fellow contributors to *Abolition Now!*] suggest that the emergence of the state-proctored non-profit industry 'suggests a historical movement away from direct, cruder forms [of state repression], toward more subtle forms of state social control of [the movement against mass incarceration].'"

Hegemony should be understood as an expression of broadly based consent, manifested in the acceptance of ideas and supported by material resources and institutions. There has been a symbiosis between corporate funders, institutions, and the state in the current campaign to co-opt the new movement against mass incarceration. The resurgent investment in prison educational funding, educational programs for the formerly incarcerated, and programs for the formerly incarcerated to enroll in higher education may be welcome in and of themselves. Yet they serve the larger purpose of the hegemony of the redemption script. Deprived of a radical critique of capitalism and its prison-industrial complex, the movement against mass incarceration runs the risk of being tamed before it has the chance to develop into a revolutionary movement for abolition as part of the struggle against the depredations of global capitalism.

Of course, co-optation of the movement against mass incarceration is the "consent" side of "consensus protected by the armor of coercion". As the state–philanthropical–corporate complex sets about its passive revolution, the nation-state is also drastically expanding its repressive apparatuses as a global police state comes into existence. Recall that a hegemonic project is constructed, in Gramsci's view, from within the *extended state*. In Gramsci's notion, this extended (or enlarged) state incorporates both political society (the state proper) and civil society. For Gramsci, "these two levels correspond on the one hand to the function of hegemony which the dominant group exercises throughout society and on the other hand to that of 'direct domination' or command exercised through the state and 'juridical' government." As social-justice struggles face off against the increasingly repressive state in this time of renewed capitalist crisis, those of us in the movement against mass incarceration must at the same time wage an uncompromising political and ideological struggle in civil society against co-optation by the redemption script.

Global capitalism post-pandemic

First published in *Race and Class*, 2020

Karl Marx and Frederick Engels famously declared in *The Communist Manifesto* that "all that is solid melts into air," under the dizzying pace of change wrought by capitalism. Not since the industrial revolution of the eighteenth century has the world experienced such rapid and profound changes as that ushered in by globalization. But now it appears that the system is at the brink of another round of restructuring and transformation based on a much more advanced digitalization of the entire global economy and society. This restructuring had already become evident in the wake of the 2008 Great Recession. But the changing social and economic conditions brought about by the coronavirus pandemic are accelerating the process. These conditions have helped a new bloc of transnational capital, led by the giant tech companies, to amass ever greater power during the pandemic and to consolidate its control over the commanding heights of the global economy. As restructuring proceeds it will heighten the concentration of capital worldwide, worsen social inequality, and aggravate international tensions. Enabled by digital applications, the ruling groups, unless they are pushed to change course by mass pressure from below, will turn to ratcheting up the global police state to contain social upheavals.

The emerging post-pandemic capitalist paradigm is based on a digitalization and application of so-called fourth industrial revolution technologies. This new wave of technological development is made possible by a more advanced information technology. Led by artificial intelligence (AI) and the collection, processing and analysis of immense amount of data ("big data"), the emerging technologies include machine learning, automation and robotics, nano- and biotechnology, the Internet of Things (IoT), quantum and cloud computing, 3D printing, virtual reality, new forms of energy storage, and autonomous vehicles, among others. Computer and information technology (CIT) first introduced in the

1980s provided the original basis for globalization. It allowed the transnational capitalist class (TCC), to coordinate and synchronize global production and therefore to put into place a globally integrated production and financial system into which every country has become incorporated. Just as the original introduction of CIT and the internet in the late twentieth century profoundly transformed world capitalism, this second generation of digital-based technologies is now leading to a new round of worldwide restructuring that promises to have another transformative impact of the structures of the global economy, society, and polity.

The first generation of capitalist globalization from the 1980s and on was based on simple digitalization - the so-called third industrial revolution. What distinguishes the fourth from the third revolution is a fusion of the new technologies and the blurring of lines between physical, digital, and biological worlds. If the first generation of capitalist globalization from the 1980s on involved the creation of a globally integrated production and financial system, the new wave of digitalization and the rise of platforms have facilitated since 2008 a very rapid transnationalization of digital-based services. By 2017 services accounted for some 70 per cent of the total gross world product and included communications, informatics, digital and platform technology, e-commerce, financial services, professional and technical work, and a host of other non-tangible products such as film and music.

It is hard to underestimate just how rapid and extensive is the current digital restructuring of the global economy and society. According to United Nations data, the "sharing economy" will surge from $14 billion in 2014 to $335 billion by 2025. Worldwide shipments of 3D printers more than doubled in 2016, to over 450, 000, and were expected to reach 6.7 million by the end of 2020. The global value of e-commerce is estimated to have reached $29 trillion in 2017, which is equivalent to 36 per cent of global gross domestic product (GDP). Digitally deliverable service exports amounted in 2019 to $2.9 trillion, or 50 per cent of global services exports. By 2019 global internet traffic was sixty-six times the volume of the entire global internet traffic in 2005, whereas Global Internet Protocol (IP) traffic, a proxy for data flows, grew from about 100 gigabytes (GB) *per day* in 1992 to more than 45,000 GB *per second* in 2017. And yet the world is only in the early days of the data-driven economy; by 2022 global IP traffic is projected to reach 150,700 GB per second, fueled by more and more people coming online for the first time and by the expansion of the IoT.

The coronavirus pandemic has spotlighted how central digital services have become to the global economy. But more than shine this spotlight, the pandemic and its aftermath, to the extent that it accelerates digital restructuring, can be expected to result in a vast expansion of reduced-labor or laborless digital services, including all sorts of new telework arrangements, drone delivery, cash-free commerce, fintech (digitalized finance), tracking and other forms of surveillance, automated medical and legal services, and remote teaching involving pre-recorded instruction. The pandemic has boosted the efforts of the giant tech companies and their political agents to convert more and more areas of the economy into these new digital realms. The giant tech companies have flourished during the contagion, their digital services becoming essential to the pandemic economy, as hundreds of millions of workers worldwide moved to remote work at home or through enhanced platforms, or became engaged in digitally-driven service work, and as in-person services were replaced by remote digital services. The post-pandemic global economy will involve now a more rapid and expansive application of digitalization to every aspect of global society, including war and repression.

New capital bloc led by tech, finance, and the military-industrial complex

Technological change is generally associated with cycles of capitalist crisis and social and political turmoil. Indeed, digitalization has been spurred on by capitalist crisis. The coronavirus was but the spark that ignited the combustible of a global economy that never fully recovered from the 2008 financial collapse and has been teetering on the brink of renewed crisis ever since. But the underlying structural causes of the 2008 debacle, far from resolved, have been steadily aggravated. Frenzied financial speculation, unsustainable debt, the plunder of public finance, overinflated tech stock, and state-organized militarized accumulation have kept the global economy sputtering along in recent years in the face of chronic stagnation and concealed its instability.

There are three types of capitalist crises. The first type is *cyclical*, or the business cycle, involving economic downturns or recessions approximately once a decade. There were recessions in the early 1980s, the early 1990s, and at the turn of the century. The second type is *structural* and appears about once every 40 to 50 years. They are called structural, or restructuring crises, because their resolution involves restructuring the capitalist system. The restructuring crisis of the late 1870s into the early 1890s was resolved through a new round of colonialism and imperialism. The 1930s Great Depression was resolved through the rise of a new type of capitalism based on redistribution and state intervention to regulate the market, known technically as Fordism-Keynesianism, and led to the social welfare systems of the twentieth century. The next structural crisis hit in the 1970s and led to globalization and the rise of a TCC from the 1980s and on. As A. Sivanandan famously noted in the late 20th century, "the handmill gives you a society with the feudal lord and the steam-mill gives you society with the industrial capitalist, the microchip gives you society with the global capitalist."

A new restructuring crisis began with the 2008 financial collapse. Leading the way in this restructuring, the giant tech companies, among them Microsoft, Apple, Amazon, Tencent, Alibaba, Facebook, and Google, and to which are now added Zoom and other companies boosted by the pandemic, have experienced astonishing growth over the past decade. Apple and Microsoft registered an astounding market capitalization of $1.4 trillion each in 2020, followed by Amazon with $1.04 trillion, Alphabet (Google's parent company) with $1.03 trillion, Samsung with $983 billion, Facebook with $604 trillion, and Alibaba and Tencent with some $500 billion each. To give an idea of just how rapidly these tech behemoths have grown, Google's market capitalization went from under $200 billion in 2008 to over one $1 trillion in 2020, or a 500 per cent increase. Meanwhile, in just two years, from 2015 to 2017, the combined value of the platform companies with a market capitalization of more than $100 million jumped by 67 per cent, to more than $7 trillion.

A handful of largely U.S.-based tech firms that generate, extract, and process data have absorbed enormous amounts of cash from transnational investors from around the world who, desperate for new investment opportunities, have poured billions of dollars into the tech and platform giants as an outlet for their surplus accumulated capital. Annual investment in CIT jumped from $17 billion in 1970, to $65 billion in 1980, then to $175 billion in 1990, $496 billion in 2000, and $654 billion in 2016, and then topped $800 billion in 2019. As capitalists invest these billions, the global banking and investment houses become interwoven with tech capital, as do businesses across the globe that are moving to cloud computing and AI. By the second decade of the century the global economy came to be characterized above all by the twin processes of digitalization and financialization.

Data shows that from the 1980s and on, those corporations that transitioned to CIT were dramatically more productive than their competitors, managing to resolve the so-called "productivity paradox," whereby the growth in productivity notably slowed from starting in 1973, the date of the onset of a structural crisis and subsequent globalization. As a result, the center of gravity in the circuits of accumulation began to shift toward those corporations developing and producing CIT. Digitalization is a "general purpose technology," meaning that, like electricity, it spreads throughout all branches of the economy and society and becomes built into everything. Those who control the development and application of digital technologies acquire newfound social power and political influence. As this process deepens, those TCC groups that control general digitalization develop new modalities for organizing the extraction of relative surplus value and increasing productivity at an exponential rate. Hence the new technologies disrupt existing value chains and generate a reorganization among sectors of capital and fractions of the capitalist class. They allow the tech giants and digitalized finance capital to appropriate ever greater shares of the value generated by global circuits of accumulation.

In this process there emerge new configurations and blocs of capital. The rise of the digital economy involves a fusion of Silicon Valley with transnational finance capital – U.S. bank investment in tech, for instance, increased by 180 per cent from 2017 to 2019 - and the military-industrial-security complex, giving rise to a new bloc of capital that appears to be at the very core of the emerging post-pandemic paradigm. This new bloc will emerge even more powerful than it was going into the health emergency, spurring a vast new centralization and concentration of capital on a global scale. At the head of this bloc, the tech behemoths are larger financial entities than most countries in the world and are able to wield enormous influence over capitalist states. New York state governor Mario Cuomo showcased this emerging capital-state relation when in early May he appointed three tech billionaires, Eric Schmidt of Google, Apple, and Facebook, former Microsoft CEO Bill Gates, and Michael Bloomberg, to head up a Blue Ribbon Commission to come up with plans to outsource public schools, hospitals, policing, and other public services to private tech companies. Such "public-private partnerships" privatize to capital traditional state functions while converting public funds into corporate subsidies.

The third leg in this triangulated bloc of capital is the military-industrial-security complex. As the tech industry emerged in the 1990s it was conjoined at birth to the military-industrial-security complex and the global police state. Over the years, for instance, Google has supplied mapping technology used by the U.S. Army in Iraq, hosted data for the Central Intelligence Agency, indexed the National Security Agency's vast intelligence databases, built military robots, co-launched a spy satellite with the Pentagon, and leased its cloud-computing platform to help police departments predict crime. Amazon, Facebook, Microsoft, and the other tech giants are thoroughly intertwined with the military-industrial and security complex. The rise of the digital economy blurs the boundaries between military and civilian sectors of the economy and brings together finance, military-industrial, and tech companies around a combined process of financial speculation and militarized accumulation.

Worldwide, total defense outlays grew by 50 per cent from 2006 to 2015, from $1.4 trillion to $2.03 trillion, although this figure does not take into account secret budgets, contingency operations, and "homeland security" spending. By 2018, private military companies employed some 15 million people around the world, while another 20 million people worked in private security. The new systems of warfare, social control, and repression are driven by digital technology. The market for new social control systems made possible by digital technology runs into the hundreds of billions. The global biometrics market, for instance, was expected to jump from its $15 billion value in 2015 to $35 billion by 2020. The concept of *militarized accumulation* helps us identify how transnational capital has become more and more dependent on a global war economy that in turn relies on perpetual state-organized war making, social control, and repression, and is driven by the new digital technologies.

Laborless production and surplus humanity

Crises provide transnational capital with the opportunity to restore profit levels by forcing greater productivity out of fewer workers. The first wave of CIT in the latter decades of the twentieth century triggered explosive growth in productivity and productive capacities, while the new digital technologies promise to multiply such capacities many times over. Specifically, digitalization vastly increases what radical political economists, following Marx, refer to as the organic composition of capital, meaning that the portion of fixed capital in the form of machinery and technology tends to increase relative to variable capital in the form of labor.

In laymen's terms, digitalization greatly accelerates the process whereby machinery and technology replace human labor, thus expanding the ranks of those who are made surplus and marginalized. One U.S. National Bureau of Economic Research report found that each new robot introduced in a locale, results in a loss of three to 5.6 jobs. In 1990 the top three carmakers in Detroit had a market capitalization of $36 billion and 1.2 million employees. In 2014 the top three firms in Silicon Valley, with a market capitalization of over $1 trillion had only 137,000 employees.

This increase in the organic composition of capital aggravates overaccumulation and social polarization, which has reached unprecedented levels worldwide. As is now well known, just one per cent of humanity owns over half of the world's wealth and the top 20 per cent own 94.5 of that wealth, while the remaining 80 per cent have to make do with just 4.5 per cent. As savage of these inequalities already were, the wealth gap widened rapidly during the pandemic, as many governments turned to massive new bailouts of capital with only modest relief, if at all, for the working classes. The U.S. and EU governments provided an astonishing $8 trillion handout to private corporations in the first two months of the pandemic alone, an amount roughly equivalent to their profits over the preceding two years. In the United States, the richest 600 billionaires increased their wealth by $700 billion from March to July 2020, even as 50 million workers lost their jobs, and as poverty, hunger, and homelessness spread. Not surprisingly, top among the earners were tech tycoons.

Such inequalities, however, end up undermining the stability of the system as the gap grows between what is (or could be) produced and what the market can absorb. The extreme concentration of the planet's wealth in the hands of the few and the accelerated impoverishment and dispossession of the majority meant that transnational capital had increasing difficulty in finding productive outlets to unload enormous amounts of surplus it accumulated. The total cash held in reserves of the world's 2,000 biggest non-financial corporations increased from $6.6 trillion in 2010 to $14.2 trillion in 2020 as the global economy stagnated. But capital cannot remain idle indefinitely without ceasing to be capital. Can the current wave of restructuring open up enough new opportunities for the TCC to invest this overaccumulated capital in the new technologies and circuits of accumulation?

The apologists of global capitalism claim that the digital economy will bring high-skilled, high-paid jobs and resolve problems of social polarization and stagnation. It is true that the first wave of digitalization in the late 20th century resulted in a bifurcation of work, generating high-paid, high-skilled jobs on one side of the pole, giving rise to new armies of tech and finance workers, engineers, software programmers, and so on. On the other side of the pole, digitalization produced a much more numerous mass of deskilled, low-wage workers and an expansion of the ranks of surplus labor. But the new wave of digitalization threatens now to make redundant much so-called "knowledge work" and to deskill and downgrade a significant portion of those knowledge-based jobs that remain. Increasingly, cognitive labor and gig workers face low wages, dull repetitive tasks, and precariousness. As "big data" captures data on knowledge-based occupations at the workplace and in the market and then converts it into algorithms, this labor itself is threatened with replacement by AI, autonomous vehicles, and the other fourth industrial revolution technologies. Digital-driven production ultimately seeks to achieve what the Nike Corporation refers to as "engineering the labor out of the product." The end game in this process, although still far away, is laborless production.

A 2017 United Nations report estimated that tens if not hundreds of millions of jobs would disappear in the coming years as a result of digitalization. As an example, the report estimated that more than 85 per cent of retails workers in Indonesia and the Philippines were at risk. The report also said that the spread of online labor platforms would accelerate a "race to the bottom of working conditions with an increasing precarity." A series of International Labor Organization (ILO) reports documented these conditions. A 1998 study found already in the late twentieth century some one-third of the global labor forces was under- or unemployed. The ILO then reported in 2011 that 1.53 billion workers around the world were in "vulnerable" employment arrangements, representing more than 50 per cent of the global workforce. Eight years later, in 2019, it concluded that a majority of the 3.5 billion workers in the world "experienced a lack of material well-being, economic security, equality opportunities or scope for human development."

Even before the pandemic hit, automation was spreading from industry and finance to all branches of services, even to fast food and agriculture. It is expected to eventually replace much professional work such as lawyers, financial analysts, doctors, journalists, accountants, insurance underwriters, and librarians. AI-driven technologies are at this time becoming more widely adopted worldwide as a result of the conditions brought about by the contagion. The pandemic allows the TCC to massively push forward capitalist restructuring that it could not previously accomplish because of resistance to the digital takeover. Those economic sectors bolstered by accelerated restructuring during the pandemic are where precarious forms of employment prevail, that is, the self-employed, contract, temporary, platform, and other such workers. There appears to be a new bifurcation of work spurred on by the pandemic, between those who will shift to remote work (more than half of all employees in the United States were working at home in May 2020, whereas worldwide, according to the ILO, some 20 per cent of employment may become permanently remote), and from their homes face new forms of control and surveillance, and those locked into high-risk "essential" in-person work, such as health care providers, cleaners, transport, and delivery workers.

Yet with heightened digitalization brought about by the pandemic there will be tens, even hundreds of millions, who lost their job but will not be reabsorbed into the labor force as technology takes over their former tasks. One University of Chicago study estimated that 42 per cent of pandemic layoffs in the United States would result in permanent job loss. As well, large corporations will snatch up millions of small businesses forced into bankruptcy (the ILO estimates that some 436 million such businesses worldwide are at risk). Capitalists will use this mass unemployment along with more widespread remote and precarious work arrangements as a lever to intensify exploitation of those with a job, to heighten discipline over the global working class, and to push surplus labor into greater marginality.

Conclusion: The fire this time

The pandemic lockdowns served as dry runs for how digitalization may allow the dominant groups to restructure space and to exercise greater control over the movement of labor. Governments around the world, from India to South Africa to El Salvador, decreed states of emergency and violently repressed those who violated stay-at-home orders. The lockdowns may have been necessary from the perspective of the health emergency. Yet they showcased how the TCC and capitalist states may more tightly control the distribution of labor power, especially surplus labor, by controlling movement and by locking labor into cyberspace and therefore making it disaggregated and isolated. As new digital technologies expand the cognitive proletariat and the ranks of workers in the gig economy they also allow for a stringent surveillance and control of this proletariat through cyberspace.

Capitalist states face spiraling crises of legitimacy after decades of hardship and social decay wrought by neoliberalism, aggravated by these states' inability to manage the health emergency and the economic collapse. In the aftermath of the pandemic there will be more inequality, conflict, militarism, and authoritarianism as social upheaval and civil strife escalate. The ruling groups will turn to expanding the global police state to contain mass discontent from below. Well before the contagion, the agents of this emerging global police state had been developing new modalities of policing and repression made possible by applications of digitalization and fourth industrial revolution technologies. These include AI powered autonomous weaponry such as unmanned attack and transportation vehicles, robot soldiers, a new generation of superdrones and flybots, hypersonic weapons, microwave guns that immobilize, cyber-attack and info-warfare, biometric identification, state data mining, and global electronic surveillance that allows for the tracking and control of every movement.

The sustained uprising in the United States (and worldwide) sparked by the May 25, 2020 police murder in the U.S. state of Minnesota of an unarmed black man, George Floyd, brought these technologies of the global police state out in full force against hundreds of thousands of anti-racist protesters across the country. State data mining and global electronic surveillance have allowed the agents of the global police state to expand theaters of conflict from active war zones to militarized cities and rural localities around the world. These combine with a restructuring of space that allow for new forms of spatial containment and control of the marginalized. We are moving toward permanent low-intensity warfare against communities in rebellion, especially racially oppressed, ethnically persecuted, and other vulnerable communities. All of this was displayed in the state repression against anti-racist protesters. Yet this low-intensity warfare is defensive, meant to disarticulate popular insurgency from below. The anti-racist uprising was the first full-scale pushback against global police state in the richest and most powerful country in the world. It hit at the jugular vein of the machinery of war and repression, giving us a glimpse of how states and ruling groups will try to ratchet up the global police state, but also how the popular majority of humanity is prepared to fight back.

There has been a rapid political polarization in global society since 2008 between an insurgent far right and an insurgent left. The ongoing crisis animates far-right and neo-fascist forces that have surged in many countries around the world and that sought to capitalize politically on the health calamity. But it also roused popular struggles from below as workers and the poor engaged in a wave of strikes and protests around the world. We have entered into a period of mounting chaos in the world capitalist system. Capitalist crises, let us recall, are times of intense social and class conflict. Depending on how these struggles play out, structural crises may expand into the third type of crisis, a *systemic* one, meaning that the crisis must be resolved by moving beyond the existing socioeconomic system, in this case capitalism.

Whether a structural crisis becomes a systemic one depends on a host of political and subjective factors than cannot be predicted beforehand. What is clear is that mass popular struggles against the depredations of global capitalism are now conjoined with those around the fallout from the health emergency. While the ruling groups deploy the new technologies to enhance their control and profit-making, this same technical infrastructure of the fourth industrial revolution is producing the resources in which a political and economic system very different from the global capitalism in which we live could be achieved. If we are to free ourselves through these new technologies, however, we would first need to overthrow the oppressive and archaic social relations of global capitalism.

The travesty of "anti-imperialism"

First published in *Journal of World-Systems Research*, 2023

In the twentieth century, the United States rose to become the leading imperialist power exercising hegemony over the world capitalist system, and became synonymous with both imperialism and capitalism. Yet world capitalism, and the international system through which it is organized, is far from static; it is in a constant state of development and change. Much of the left seems incapable of conceptualizing the transformations that have occurred in these recent decades of capitalist globalization, instead clinging tenaciously to an ossified formula of a singular U.S. empire, with the triad countries in tow and the rest of the world victims of this empire. In this formula, anything that seems to challenge the Sole Enemy is seen as progressive, part of a just struggle of the oppressed, and deserving of support. As a result, a self-declared "anti-imperialist" left condemns capitalist exploitation and repression around the world when it is practiced by the United States and other Western powers or the governments they support, yet turns a blind eye to (or even defends) repressive, authoritarian, and dictatorial states simply because these states face hostility from Washington.

There are two stories here. One involves a political critique of this "anti-imperialism" logic. The other is how concepts and practices that were historically part of the left and progressive social change agendas – solidarity, sovereignty, and proletarian internationalism – have been redefined to justify exploitation and repression.

The politics of capitalist exploitation and social control around the world are fundamentally shaped by the contradiction between a globally integrated economy and a nation-state-based system of political domination. Economic globalization and the transnational integration of capitals provide a centripetal impulse to global capitalism, whereas political fragmentation gives a powerful centrifugal counterimpulse that is resulting in an escalation of geopolitical conflict. The chasm is rapidly widening between the economic unity of global capital, and political competition among ruling groups who must achieve legitimacy and keep the internal social order of their respective nations from fracturing in the face of the escalating crisis of global capitalism. States attempt to shift the burden of the crisis onto the working and popular classes, as governments turn to more repressive, authoritarian, and even fascist forms of rule, and to diverse ideological and rhetorical devices, to contain mass unrest. The effort requires sublimating and externalizing social and political tensions onto political rivals, more peripheral regions, and vulnerable groups or external enemies that may be conjured up when none exist. The more powerful a state, the more advantage it has in these efforts.

This global conjuncture is the backdrop to a contemporary "socialism of fools." I will discuss here the cases of Nicaragua and the BRICS (Brazil, Russia, India, China, South Africa), especially China, and multipolarity as they bring out the convoluted logic and retrograde politics of the "anti-imperialist" left.

China and capitalist development

China now has, by a long chalk, more billionaires than the United States: 969 to 691.

Inequality in China surpassed that of the United States by a large margin a decade ago, and the country is now one of the most unequal in the world. Capitalism with Chinese characteristics has involved the rise of powerful Chinese transnational capitalists fused with a state-party elite dependent on the reproduction of capital, and high-consumption middle strata, fueled by a devastating wave of primitive accumulation in the countryside and the exploitation of hundreds of millions of Chinese workers. Marx had defined socialism as the emancipatory self-activity of the workers. Yet strikes and independent unions are not legal in China. The Chinese Communist Party has long since abandoned any talk of class struggle or workers' power. As labor struggles continue to escalate in the country, so too does state repression of them.

It is true that capitalist development in China has lifted millions out of extreme poverty – at least according to the narrow World Bank measurements of poverty as below $785 in annual income – even as the "iron rice bowl" that guaranteed lifetime employment and welfare was abandoned three decades ago. This development has brought about rapid industrialization, technological progress, and advanced infrastructure. It is equally true that the North American and Western European core countries experienced these achievements during their periods of rapid capitalist development from the late nineteenth to the mid-twentieth centuries. The left never saw this capitalist development in the West as a victory for the working class, nor did it lose sight of the link between this development, the law of combined and uneven accumulation in the larger world capitalist system, and plunder abroad that made this development possible. China is now "catching up." If colonial conquest and the transfer of surplus back to the traditional core played a major role in raising living standards in the West, the Chinese revolution of 1949, with its destruction of the atavistic classes, made possible rapid capitalist development once China opened up in the 1980s.

The Chinese state-capitalist model rests on a complex of state-private companies in which private capital accounts for three-fifths of output and four-fifths of urban employment. China may represent the future not of "socialism" but of global capitalism. China has not followed the neoliberal route to transnational capitalist integration. The state plays a key role in the financial system, in regulating private capital, in massive public expenditure, especially in infrastructure, and in planning. This has allowed it to develop twenty-first century infrastructure, to undertake cutting edge research and development, and to guide capital accumulation into aims broader than that of immediate profit-making. This model of capitalist development may be distinct from the Western neoliberal variant, but it still obeys the laws of capital accumulation. Following the opening to global capitalism in the 1980s, China became a market for transnational corporations and a sink for surplus accumulated capital that was able to take advantage of a vast supply of cheap labor, controlled by a repressive, omnipresent surveillance state. But by the turn of the century, pressures were building up to find outlets abroad for surplus Chinese capital that was accumulated during years of hothouse capitalist development.

The sustaining of this development in China now became dependent on the export of capital abroad, not unlike how over-accumulated capital in Europe turned to a fresh round of imperialism in the late nineteenth century in order to open up new outlets for unloading surplus and for procuring raw materials, labor, and markets. China and other states in the former Third World do not need to undertake colonial conquest at this time in order to export capital, exploit labor, and access markets abroad, as the task of violently integrating all countries into world capitalism was already accomplished by the West in previous centuries. In the first two decades of the twenty-first century, China led the world in a surge of outward foreign direct investment (FDI) to countries in the global South and North alike, deepening transnational integration and accelerating capitalist transformation. Between 1991 and 2003, China's FDI increased tenfold, and then increased 13.7 times from 2004 to 2013, from $45 billion to $613 billion. By 2015, China had become the third-largest foreign investor in the world. Its outbound FDI began to exceed inbound FDI and the country became a net creditor. What happens when this Chinese outward FDI touches down in the former Third World?

Displacement and extraction become "South–South co-operation"

In recent years, the indigenous communities of the Peruvian highland province of Apurímac have waged bloody struggles that have left scores dead and injured against the Las Bambas open-pit copper mine, one of the largest in the world. The mine has been owned and operated since 2014 by the Chinese state-private transnational mining conglomerate MMG. (The 25 per cent that is private includes global investor groups.) In 2022, the Peruvian government approved the mine's expansion, violently evicting indigenous communities that had blocked roads and camped on mine property. In fact, the Peruvian state legally sells policing services to mining companies, enabling MMG to purchase physical force from the police to advance copper extraction by violent means.

While this Sino-Peruvian extractive space and others like it are touted by the Chinese as models of South–South co-operation and post-Western modernization, keen observers will recognize at once the classical structure of imperialist extraction. Transnational capital displaces communities and appropriates resources, under the political and military protection of local states who are tasked with the violent repression of resistance to expulsion and exploitation. But because investors are (mostly) Chinese, not Western, they escape condemnation by the "anti-imperialist" left that has historically been trained to recognize such actions as imperialism only when carried out by Western states.

Extractive activity by transnational capital requires logistical infrastructure such as roads, railroads, ports, and dams for the supply of energy. There is a well-known history of World Bank and other Western finance for megaprojects that facilitate the inward penetration of transnational capital, the extraction of raw materials and industrial goods, the opening up of markets, and the global movement of capital and profits. Dependency theorist André Gunder Frank noted long ago how value first extracted in hinterlands passes through scalar networks, which serve as arteries for the progressive movement of these values from more peripheral to more core regions and groups within and among countries. Alongside MMG and other Chinese mining and industrial transnationals, the Chinese state-owned conglomerate Cosco Shipping Holdings, in collaboration with the Swiss-based company Glencore, is building a megaport and industrial zone on the Peruvian coast, along with railroads leading inland to agro-industrial and mining zones. This is part of China's Belt and Roads initiative, a global infrastructure plan to open up markets and boost international trade and investment routes. As with Las Bambas, local communities in Chancay, fifty miles north of Peru's capital, Lima, have been battling displacement, takeover by private companies, and environmental destruction.

The pattern is the same throughout Latin America. Workers, peasants, and indigenous communities have no say whatsoever in these projects; they are decided on and imposed by local states in collusion with transnational capital. Chinese banks have given out more than $137 billion in loans to finance infrastructure, energy, and mining projects in the region. One 2022 report by a coalition of environmental and human rights groups in Latin America looked at 26 projects in Argentina, Bolivia, Brazil, Chile, Colombia, Ecuador, Mexico, Peru, and Venezuela. It found widespread violations of human rights, the displacement of local communities, environmental devastation, and violent conflict wherever Chinese investment in mines and megaprojects took place. Defenders of loan practices by China claim that these loans are different from those coming from the West because they do not impose conditionality in the way that Western lenders do. This is not entirely true. But even if it were, what difference does that make for workers and peasants resisting the exploitation, repression, and environmental destruction associated with Chinese investments in collaboration with transnational investors from elsewhere and local capitalist states?

The point is not that Chinese capital is worse or better than capital originating from other countries. Capital is capital irrespective of the national identity or ethnicity of its bearers. However, when a Western capitalist state and a capitalist state in the global South co-operate to impose megaprojects on local communities or to facilitate transnational corporate plunder in extraction or industry, this is condemned as exploitation by imperialism and local ruling classes. When two capitalist states from the global South co-operate for the same megaprojects and corporate exploitation, this is praised as progressive, anti-imperialist "South–South co-operation" and "bringing development." Yet proletarian internationalism calls on us to support the struggle of working and popular classes against the control and exploitation by capital, irrespective of the nationality of the capital.

Capitalist development is not a class-neutral process. It is by definition a class project of the bourgeoisie. One may argue that development must still take place even if it is capitalist, and that such infrastructure is necessary for development. But then, why not applaud the megaprojects, extractivism, and maquiladoras coming from Western capitalists and states? Are we really to believe that Chinese investors are rapidly setting up export-processing zones and relocating labor-intensive industrial production from China to lower-wage zones in Ethiopia, Vietnam, and elsewhere, not to make profit but to "help these countries develop"? Is that not the same legitimating discourse as that of the World Bank?

Such outfits as the Tricontinental, headed by Vijay Prashad, consistently gush praise on this Chinese role in the former Third World as "mutually beneficial," "helping development," and a "win–win" for China and the countries its corporations invest in. Parroting the legitimating discourse of the Chinese state-party elite, the Tricontinental has also insisted that "the peaceful rise of socialism with Chinese characteristics" provides an alternative to Western imperialism. Well, it does. But not an alternative to capitalist dispossession and exploitation. Capitalist development, whether from the West or the East, is about expanding the frontiers of accumulation. Those who cheerlead China remain silent on two counts: first, on the Chinese state's defense of capital and repression of the Chinese working class inside the country, and second, on its capitalist exploitation abroad.

The misuse of sovereignty and solidarity

The "anti-imperialist" left rightfully decries Western propaganda, but seems incapable of calling out or even recognizing non-Western propaganda around the world – or worse yet, parrots that same propaganda. Sometimes the slightest rhetorical "anti-imperialist" flush from a country's head of state – often directed at maintaining an internal base of support – will whip the myopic into action in defense of a state, regardless of the nature of the regime in question. Nicaragua provides a textbook case. The Ortega regime has proved remarkably adroit at using radical-sounding language and anti-imperialist rhetoric to strike a reflexive chord of support among the international left. Yet there is an utter non-correspondence between this rhetoric and the reality in the country.

Ortega returned to power in 2007 through a pact with the country's traditional right-wing oligarchy, the former members of the armed counter-revolution (known as the contras), and the conservative Catholic Church hierarchy and Evangelical sects. Promising absolute respect for private property and unrestricted freedom for capital, he then proceeded to cogovern with the capitalist class, granting transnational capital ten-year across-the-board tax holidays, deregulation, unrestricted freedom to repatriate profits, neoliberal policies, and repression of striking workers and peasants. Banking, agriculture, industry, imports, and exports are all controlled by local and transnational capitalist conglomerates. (Ninety-six per cent of the country's property remains in the hands of the private sector.) The dictatorship has repressed all dissent and shut down over 3,500 civil society organizations – this in a country of barely six million people – because it considers *any* civic life outside of its own to be a threat.

Many progressives may be genuinely confused because of the well-deserved support that the 1979–1990 Sandinista revolution marshaled around the world, and the history of brutal U.S. intervention in that country. That revolution died in 1990 and what came to power in 2007 under Ortega was anything but revolution. Yet the "anti-imperialist" left has chosen to warmly embrace the dictatorship, justified by alleged U.S. attempts to destabilize the regime, and in the name of "sovereignty." But the evidence does not support the claim made by these detractors that the United States is pushing "counter-revolutionary regime change" against Ortega, notwithstanding Washington's saber-rattling rhetoric.

Nicaragua does not face trade or investment sanctions. The United States is the country's principal trading partner – bilateral trade surpassed $8.3 billion in 2022 – and transnational corporate investment continues to pour in, as does multilateral lending to the Central Bank (following a January 2023 visit to the country, the IMF reiterated its longstanding praise for the government's neoliberal policies). There is no military or paramilitary aggression. In fact, until 2018 Washington routinely commended Ortega for his close co-operation with the U.S. Southern Command, the Drug Enforcement Agency, and U.S. immigration policy. Yet none of these facts stopped the U.S.-based organization Code Pink, among others, from claiming that Ortega's is a "socialist government" under pressure from "devastating sanctions" and facing "violent attempted coups."

The claim by the "anti-imperialists" to be defending Nicaragua's sovereignty rings utterly hollow, considering that Ortega is responsible for the single biggest giveaway of sovereignty in the country's history when in 2013 it granted a concession to the Hong Kong-based company HKND, headed by the Chinese billionaire Wang Jing, to build and run a canal from the country's Caribbean to Pacific coasts. Law 480 granted HKND exclusive concessions for fifty years, and the option to extend them for another fifty years. It included a concession for carrying out seven subprojects – among them ports, oil pipelines, free-trade zones, and tourist areas – that could be carried out in any part of the national territory under the control of the concessionaire. Although construction of the canal has yet to commence because of HKND's financial problems, the project has already resulted in vast land expropriations and the estimates of how many would be displaced should the project proceed run up to one hundred thousand people.

Washington does wage full-blown destabilization campaigns against Iran, Venezuela, and other countries. Such crimes must be vehemently condemned by any leftist worthy of the name. But this does not absolve the left of its ethical and political commitment to internationalism and solidarity with those oppressed, just because we resist U.S. imperial pretensions around the world. The "anti-imperialist" left, however, will tell you otherwise. Heed the warning of journalist Caitlin Johnstone: if you live in a Western country, "it is simply is not possible for you to lend your voice to the cause of protesters in empire-targeted nations without facilitating the empire's propaganda campaigns about those protests. You either have a responsible relationship with this reality or an irresponsible one." Simple as that. Proletarians of just *some* countries, unite!

Sovereignty originally referred to the total domination of a supreme authority, derived from the Roman *summum imperium* (the highest authority) and *merum imperium* (unqualified authority). This conception reached its apogee in the age of European absolutism and in pre-capitalist dynastic and imperial systems around the world. The French Revolution counterposed the supreme power of states to the bourgeois conception of the "general will," followed later by that of "popular sovereignty" as the principle of democratic control by the people, along with the principle of non-interference in the internal affairs of states (this latter being falsely credited to the 1648 Treaty of Westphalia).

While we can appreciate how the institutions of bourgeois democracy help to secure the illusion of consent under the cloak of hegemony, the dimwitted seem to have reverted to the conception of absolute sovereignty, *not* of the people or the working classes, but of the rulers in countries that the "anti-imperialists" defend. Not the sovereignty of the Nicaraguan people, but the absolute sovereignty of the Ortega dictatorship. Not the sovereignty of the Chinese people, but the absolute sovereignty of the Chinese state and Community Party. This confusion of the sovereignty of nations and peoples with that of states was brought home in one recent article by Alex Rubinstein, a writer for the *Grayzone*. The United States, he contended, was intervening in Syria to lay claim to Syrian oil. This contention was followed by a woefully revealing political Freudian slip: Syrian oil "rightfully belongs to the sovereign government of Syria."

Anti-colonial and anti-imperialist struggles in the twentieth century defended *national* – not *state* – sovereignty in the face of interference by the colonial and imperial powers. Capitalist states use this claim to sovereignty as a "right" to exploit and oppress inside national borders, free from outside interference. The systematic violation of human rights is not covered by the principle in international law of nonintervention in the internal affairs of nations. We on the left have no qualms about "violating national sovereignty" to condemn human rights abuses by pro-Western regimes, and nor should we in defense of human rights under those regimes not favored by Washington.

Proletarian internationalism calls on the working and oppressed classes of one country to extend solidarity not to states, but to the struggles of the working and oppressed classes of other countries. For the "anti-imperialists", if you are oppressed and exploited by a government that the Washington backs then your struggle is worthy of support; otherwise, you are a lackey of imperialism. States deserve the left's support to the extent – and only to the extent – that they advance the emancipatory struggles of the popular and working classes; that they advance, or are forced to advance, policies that favor these classes. The "anti-imperialists" conflate state with nation, country, and people, generally lacking any theoretical conception of these categories and advancing a populist over a class political orientation. We on the left condemned the U.S. invasion and occupation of Iraq earlier this century. We did so not because we supported the Saddam Hussein regime – only a fool could have – but because we stood in solidarity with the Iraqi people and because the whole imperial project for the Middle East was tantamount to an attack on the poor and the oppressed everywhere.

BRICS: replacing the capital-labor contradiction with a North-South contradiction

The "anti-imperialists" cheer on the BRICS bloc of nations (Brazil, Russia, India, China, South Africa) as a Southern challenge to global capitalism: a progressive, even anti-imperialist option for humanity. They can only make such a claim by reducing capitalism and imperialism to Western supremacy in the international system. In this realist worldview, the struggle of workers and the oppressed is here transmuted into the struggle among capitalist states for political hegemony in inter-state relations.

In the heyday of colonialism and its immediate aftermath, local ruling classes in the former Third World were, at best, anti-imperialist but not anti-capitalist. Their nationalism obliterated class by proclaiming an identity of interests among the citizens of a particular country. This nationalism had a progressive and sometimes even radical edge to it, so far as all members of the country in question were oppressed by colonial domination, the caste systems it imposed, and the suppression of indigenous capital. Today's "anti-imperialists" wax enthusiasm for the BRICS as a revived "Third World project," in the words of Vijay Prashad, as little more than antiquated nostalgia for that anti-colonial moment of the mid-twentieth century. Two references will suffice to illustrate just how out of touch such thinking is with the twenty-first-century reality.

A number of years ago I had the opportunity to give a talk in Manila to a group of Philippine revolutionary activists. One woman in attendance, originally from India, objected to my analysis of the rise of a transnational capitalist class that incorporated powerful contingents from the former Third World. Visibly disturbed, she told me that in India "we are fighting against imperialism and for national liberation, just as Lenin had analyzed." I asked her what she meant by this. The core countries were exploiting Indian workers and transferring the surplus back to the imperialist countries, she replied. It was by sheer coincidence that in the very week of my talk, the Indian-based global corporate conglomerate, the Tata Group, which operates in over a hundred countries in six continents, had acquired a string of corporate icons of its former British colonial master, among them, Land Rover, Jaguar, Tetley Tea, British Steel, and Tesco supermarkets. This made Tata the single largest employer *inside* the United Kingdom. So India-based capitalists had become the largest single exploiter of British workers. According to this woman's own outdated logic, the United Kingdom was now the victim of Indian imperialism!

Meanwhile, shortly after his first inauguration, in 2003, and then again in 2010 during his second presidential term, Brazilian President Lula loaded up a government aircraft with Brazilian corporate executives and headed for Africa. The presidential-corporate entourage lobbied Mozambique and other African countries to open up to investment in the continent's abundant mineral resources by the Brazilian-based transnational mining corporation Vale, under the rhetoric of "South–South solidarity." It is unclear what was anti-imperialist, much less anti-capitalist, about Lula's African corporate safaris, and by extension the "South–South co-operation" agenda it epitomized, or why the left should be applauding the expansion of Brazilian-based capital into Africa, Chinese-based capital into Latin America, Russian-based capital into Central Asia, or Indian-based capital into the United Kingdom.

As Franz Fanon famously noted in *The Wretched of the Earth*, the national bourgeoisies of the former Third World were born decadent and treacherous. Far from challenging these bourgeoisies, the BRICS governments facilitate the expansion of transnational capital and the ongoing integration of "their" national bourgeoisies into now-globalized circuits of accumulation. It is therefore not just that the leading capitalist strata from the historic periphery have transnationalized across the South and the North, but that in doing so, they have integrated into a global ruling class that exercises its power over the laboring masses in *both* South *and* North. The principal contradiction worldwide now is between global capital and global labor. The romantic yearning for a new Third World project obscures internal class contradictions, along with the web of transnational class relations into which they are enmeshed.

We may support the (mildly) redistributive policies at home, and dynamic foreign policy abroad, of governments such as Lula's. All capitalist states are not the same, and it matters a great deal who is in the government. But a "progressive" government is not a socialist and not necessarily an anti-imperialist government. For the myopic, the outward expansion of Chinese, Indian, or Brazilian-based capital is seen as some sort of liberation from imperialism. What is one to make of the bizarre claim by the Canadian-based "anti-imperialist" Geopolitical Economy Research Group, and the International Manifesto Group that it sponsors, for whom ideological commitment trumps facts, that the BRICS are "among the better-known successes" in efforts to promote "autonomous and egalitarian national development and industrialization to break imperialist shackles"?

If the BRICS do not represent an alternative to global capitalism and the domination of transnational capital, they *do* signal the shift toward a more multipolar and balanced *inter-state* system *within* the global capitalist order. But such a multipolar inter-state system remains part of a brutal, exploitative, global capitalist world, in which the BRICS capitalists and states are as much committed to control and exploitation of the global working and popular classes as are their Northern counterparts. As the BRICS membership expands, new candidates in 2023 to join the bloc include such magnificently "autonomous and egalitarian" states fighting "imperialist shackles" as Saudi Arabia, Egypt, Bahrain, Afghanistan, Nigeria, and Kazakhstan.

Multipolarity: the new albatross

The 2022 Russian invasion of Ukraine and the West's radical political, military, and economic response to it may signal the *coup de grace* of a decadent post-WWII international order. The prevailing distribution of formal decision-making power among states in this post-War order does not reflect radical changes in recent decades in the relative weight of states in the international system. An ever more integrated global capitalism is inconsistent with a U.S.- and Western-controlled international political order and financial architecture, and with an exclusively dollar-denominated global economy. We are at the onset of a radical reconfiguration of global geopolitical alignments to the drumbeat of escalating economic turbulence and political chaos. Yet the crisis of hegemony in the international order takes place within this single, integrated global economy.

The emerging global capitalist pluralism may offer greater maneuvering room for popular struggles around the world, but a politically multipolar world does not mean that emerging poles of global capitalism are any less exploitative or oppressive than the established centers. The limits to this maneuvering room were made clear in the May 2023 announcement by the Russian magnate Boris Titov, who heads the Russia–Cuba Business Council, that Russian capitalists would invest in Cuba thanks to generous concessions, including thirty-year land concessions, tax exemptions on machinery imports, and the repatriation of profits. However, as part of any investment deal, Titov explained, "we would like to see new measures as well. The issue of tax preferences, an independent personnel policy of Russian employers in Cuba, including the right to freely hire and dismiss employees [that is, a capitalist labor market with no state protection], and preferential access of Russian companies to public procurement [of state contracts]. We hope that in the near future ... the whole range of preferences will be enshrined into law."

To the contrary, the established West and the emerging centers in this polycentric world are converging around remarkably similar "Great Power" tropes, especially jingoistic – often ethnic – nationalism and nostalgia for a mythologized "glorious civilization" that must now be rejuvenated. The Spenglerian narrative differs from one country to another according to particular histories and cultures. In China, hyper-nationalism combines with Confucian obedience to authority, Han ethnic supremacy, and a new Long March to recover great power status. For Putin, it is the glory days of a "Great Russia" empire anchored in Eurasia, politically propped up by extreme patriarchal conservatism that Putin calls "traditional spiritual and moral values" embodying the "spiritual essence of the Russian nation over the decaying West." In the United States, it is the hyper-imperial bravado of a waning Pax Americana legitimated by the doctrine of "U.S. exceptionalism" and the bombast of "democracy and freedom," at whose fringe has always been white supremacy, now incarnated in a rising fascist movement as "replacement theory." To these we could add pan-Turkism, Hindu nationalism, and other such quasi-fascist ideologies in this rising polycentric world. Make America Great Again! Make China Great Again! Make Russia Great Again!

The United States may be the top dog and the most dangerous criminal among competing cartels of criminal states. We must condemn Washington for instigating a New Cold War and for prodding Russia through aggressive NATO expansion into invading Ukraine. Yet the "anti-imperialist" left insists that there is one Single Enemy: the United States and its allies. This is a Manichean tale of "the West and the rest." Such a metaphysical *Star Wars* narrative about the virtuous fight against the singular Evil Empire ends up legitimating the Russian invasion of Ukraine, as if one crime justifies another. And just as in *Star Wars*, it becomes hard to distinguish the fanciful babble of a fantasy world from the babble of the "anti-imperialist" left.

Capitalist globalization, transnational class exploitation, and the global police state

An interview with William I. Robinson

First published in LINKS, International Journal of Socialist Renewal, *2023*

LINKS: Over the past century, we have seen the term "imperialism" used to define different situations and at other times be replaced by concepts such as globalization and hegemony. You yourself have written that "the classical image of imperialism as a relation of external domination is outdated." Why is this the case? Does this mean the concept of imperialism as a whole is outdated too? How best then can we understand global capitalism today?

William I. Robinson (WIR): Colonialism and imperialism are historic processes through which world capitalism expanded outward from its original birthplace in Western Europe and conquered the world. Capitalism is by its very nature an outwardly expanding system. It must continuously conquer new spaces and expand the frontiers of accumulation, commodify everything, obliterate all that stands in its way. By imperialism we mean this violent outward expansion of capital, with all the political, military, and ideological mechanisms that this involves. Given the profound transformations in world capitalism over the past half decade, it could not be clearer that we need to reconceive how we understand imperialism in this age of capitalist globalization.

Lenin argued in *Imperialism: The Highest Stage of Capitalism*, written in the midst of the First World War, that the conflagration had to be understood as a battle among European states for colonial zones of influence to secure, in competition with rival states, raw materials, labor pools, markets, and outlets for surplus accumulated capital. He was clear that this conflict among states expressed a more fundamental, underlying conflict among nationally organized capitalist classes and therefore the essence of imperialism was rivalry among these national capitalist classes for world control.

But Lenin was analyzing world capitalism at an earlier moment in its ongoing and open-ended evolution in which capitalist classes were organized nationally. The world he and his generation of Marxist revolutionaries looked out upon was very different than the world we now live in. The idea predominant among leftists at this time is that Lenin advanced a nation-state or territorially-based theory of imperialism. This is fundamentally wrong. He advanced a *class-based* theory. A nation cannot exploit another nation – that is just so much absurd reification. Imperialism has always been a violent class relation, not between countries but between global capital and global labor, a *class project* mediated, however, through a world economy politically divided into national jurisdictions.

Our challenge as Marxists is to understand the changing relationship between class (and capital) and state in the context of transnational class exploitation. The worldwide organization of capital has changed over the past century through the transnationalization of the leading fractions of capital. This has been so broadly documented empirically that it should no longer be controversial. The transnational capitalist class (TCC) as the hegemonic fraction of capital on a world scale is not tethered to territory and while it has to rely on and also contend with states it does not identify with any one nation-state.

But transnational capital is not just "Northern" or "triad" capital. It includes the rise of powerful transnational corporate conglomerates from the formerly colonized countries that now export their capital around the world in the same way as European imperial powers did in Lenin's day. The Brazilian-based transnational conglomerate, Vale, one of the world's largest integrated mining companies, ceased being a "Brazilian" company in the twenty-first century. It has operations on every continent and exploits tens of thousands of workers in the traditional North American and European core. But there are countless other examples. The Indian-based Tata conglomerate is the single largest employer (and therefore capitalist exploiter of labor) in the United Kingdom. Chinese-based corporations operate in every continent, including in North America, where they exploit U.S. and Canadian workers. Mexican-based transnationals invest throughout Latin and North America and beyond, exploiting workers of all nationalities. Gulf-based capitalists export capital around the world. Moreover, when we set about to analyze the structure of global capital we find a very high degree of transnational integration, especially through the circuits of global finance and cross-corporate investment.

Imperialism in the economic sense has historically referred to the appropriation of resources and the exploitation of labor across national borders and the flow of the surplus value therein extracted back across borders. Now this takes place all over the world. It does not resemble the earlier structure in which metropolitan colonial capital simply siphoned out surplus value from the colonies and deposited it back in colonial coffers.

There is nothing intrinsically – as distinct from historically – Western about imperialism. It historically had a Western identity because capitalism was born in the West and expanded out from there. We are now in a new epoch of global capitalism. Many Marxists lose sight of the fact that historically imperialism refers to an economic relationship facilitated by extra-economic (political, military, etc.) processes. They focus on the extra-economic processes alone, such as U.S. interventionism around the world, without showing their relationship to transnational class exploitation as it actually takes place. For instance, the United States props up repressive governments in Latin America whereas in these same countries Chinese or other transnational investors exploit labor but do not intervene politically to prop up repressive states. What is the relationship here between U.S. intervention and Chinese capitalist exploitation? As socialists shouldn't we be opposing not just the political (and sometimes military) intervention but also the class exploitation that it makes possible?

It is through a globally integrated production, financial, and service system that global capital controls resources and exploits global labor. How can we understand the political and military processes that facilitate these worldwide relations of exploitation? As socialists we oppose imperialism because it is the vehicle of barbarous capitalist dispossession, exploitation, oppression, and degradation. We cannot oppose imperialism while embracing or excusing capitalist exploitation. I am still sifting through these matters and don't have all the answers. But it is clear that we need a very great deal of rethinking and there is just so much I can say here.

LINKS: You have written about the emergence of a TCC. How do you see the relation between this class and nation-states evolving? Can this TCC operate successfully without an institutional anchorage in, and political backing from, an imperialist power?

WIR: Capital cannot reproduce or expand without the state. That has been true throughout the whole history of world capitalism and remains true today. In this age of globalization, the world has to be pried open to transnational capital and then kept open to it. All threats to its freedom to exploit and accumulate have to be suppressed. How is this to be achieved? It requires political, military, and economic instruments, ranging from coups d'état and military interventions, to economic sanctions, structural adjustment programs, free-trade agreements, the mechanisms of debt and financial leverage, lawfare, and so on. In speaking about the TCC's anchorage in states, we need to focus on two aspects: first, how the TCC has sought to impose its class power over the past four decades of capitalist globalization through a dense network of national and supra national institutions around the world, and second, the preponderant role to date of the U.S. state in capitalist globalization.

Regarding the first, as far back as the 1970s, with the formation of the Trilateral Commission and the World Economic Forum, an emerging transnational elite sought to develop transnational networks to coordinate policy and impose worldwide the conditions for capitalist globalization. I have put forth the concept of transnational states (TNS) apparatuses, *not* as a "world government" but as an analytical abstraction that refers to the loose networks of inter- and transnational institutions *together with* national states through which the TCC attempts to exercise its class power over the global working classes leveraging the structural power of transnational capital over the direct power of states. I have discussed these matters broadly and cannot reiterate them here. But let's note, for instance, that when the IMF imposes as a condition for a loan that local labor markets be deregulated, or fiscal austerity so as to assure the macroeconomic stability that transnational finance requires, the IMF is acting as a (transnational) state institution insofar as the capitalist state establishes the conditions for exploitation to take place, in this case within the larger global capitalist system.

Regarding the second, most Marxists today assume that U.S. intervention and aggression around the world – if we want to call this imperialism, fine, but not without qualification – should be understood as competition with other powers. But let us recall that the British and the French sealed off their colonial empires in earlier centuries to capitalists from other countries, whereas U.S.-led capitalist globalization has sought in recent decades to open up the world to capital from all over irrespective of national origin. When the U.S. invaded and occupied Iraq in the early 21st century it opened up the country to investors from all over the world. In fact, the first two oil conglomerates that took advantage of the U.S. military canopy to invest in Iraqi oil fields were the French-based Total and the Chinese state oil company, even though the French and Chinese governments opposed the invasion. Chinese private and state corporations control most of the production of cobalt in the Congo (in the process brutally exploiting Congolese miners and plundering the country). That cobalt goes back to industrial circuits in Asia where iPhones and other electronic equipment is manufactured by transnational capital and marketed around the world.

Phrases such as "national interests" (as in "defending U.S. interests") are meaningless and have no place in Marxist analysis. What we really mean to ask is, what are the *class interests* behind what the U.S. state does around the world? The U.S. state has served over the past four decades as the imperial anchor to which you refer, as the most powerful instrument in the arsenal of global capitalism through which the mass of the world's poor and working peoples are contained and controlled, the world is further pried open for transnational corporate plunder, and states that impede the unfettered accumulation of capital are attacked.

Now, however, things are changing rapidly. There is a general crisis of capitalist rule. Any effort at transnational capitalist unity is undermined by the escalating crisis of global capitalism. TNS apparatuses are breaking down. The World Trade Organization trade rules are being disregarded by the very U.S. national state that so forcefully pushed for them at the height of neoliberal globalization. Escalating geopolitical conflict has more to do with challenges to the global capitalist order and to competition among state elites as they face mounting crises of accumulation, political legitimacy, social reproduction, and control than with competition among national capitalist groups. No one national state, no matter how powerful, has the ability to serve at this time as the anchorage that you ask about, to stabilize the global economy or control global accumulation. We are in a period of global chaos without a coherent political center to stabilize global capitalism.

LINKS: In light of the changes experienced during the past century, what relative weight do the mechanisms of imperialist exploitation (unequal exchange, enforced subordination to the economic interests of the imperialist centers, military blackmail, economic sanctions, etc.) have today, as compared to the past?

WIR: This is a very important question. World capitalism is still organized through an international division of labor and a center-peripheral structure of transnational class relations forged through the centuries of colonialism and imperialism. Labor is more intensely exploited in the former Third World and the absolute savagery of capital more fully on display. But here is the key point: most on the left see the greater intensity of exploitation, or what some Marxist theorists describe as super-exploitation, as something that benefits only capitalists from core countries, or worst still, they see it has something that benefits nations.

But who is superexploiting workers in the former Third World? Most on the left see the exploiter as an "imperialist nation." This is a reification insofar as nations are not and have never been macro-agents. A nation cannot exploit or be exploited; classes exploit and are exploited. With the rise of powerful contingents of the TCC in many countries of the former Third World, transnational capitalists from all over the world are able to take advantage of the conditions of super-exploitation where those conditions exist. Transnational capitalists from Mexico, Brazil, Argentina, India, Nigeria, and so on – from supposedly "oppressed nations" - are able to super-exploit workers in their own and in each other's countries, just as capitalists from the U.S., EU or elsewhere are able to. In other words, it is not (or no longer) just core-based capitalists who, in pursuing accumulation strategies, benefit from the combined and uneven accumulation of capital on a world scale and distinct spaces and political jurisdictions. The relationship of the core-periphery structure of the world economy to global capitalism cannot be understood in terms that correspond to earlier centuries, and especially not in terms of some bourgeoisie in peripheral regions oppressed by metropolitan capital and prepared to join class alliances with workers and peasants of the countries where they (but not necessarily their capital) reside.

On the other hand, states in the former Third World have to manage the tensions and conflicts of underdevelopment and the more acute inequalities and deprivations as well as sharper social conflict that it involves. More powerful states of the traditional core are better equipped to displace the acute contradictions of the crisis to countries in the historic periphery. However, transnational capital is an internal class relation around the world. The global capital–labor contradiction undergirds the "North–South" contradiction.

LINKS: In your writings you have referred to the rise of a global police state that is increasingly dependent on militarized accumulation. Could you outline what you mean by this?

WIR: The global police state refers to the ever more ubiquitous systems of warfare, mass social control, surveillance and repression to contain the global working classes and criminalize surplus humanity at a time when worldwide inequalities and mass deprivation have never been so acute, when the ranks of surplus labor are swelling exponentially, and when popular rebellion is breaking out everywhere. The ruling groups are turning toward authoritarianism, dictatorship, and even fascism as consensual mechanisms of domination break down. States may be in fierce competition over expanding the frontiers of global accumulation yet every capitalist on the planet needs a global police state to control and discipline the working and popular classes while every capitalist state serves this mandate.

But global police state also refers to militarized accumulation and accumulation by repression. The political goal of control and domination come together with the economic goal of accumulation. The problem of surplus capital is endemic to capitalism but over the past couple of decades it has reached extraordinary levels. The TCC has been in a desperate search for outlets to unload its surplus accumulated surplus. Historically wars have provided critical economic stimulus and served as outlets for surplus accumulated capital but there is something qualitatively new going on now with global police state. As I showed in my 2020 book, *The Global Police State*, the global economy has become deeply dependent on the development and deployment of systems of warfare, social control and repression as a means of making profit and continuing to accumulate capital in the face of chronic stagnation and the saturation of global markets.

In recent decades states have seen an unprecedented fusion of private accumulation with state militarization. The so-called wars on drugs and terrorism and the mass control of immigrant and refugee populations, mass incarceration, border walls, and so on, are enormously profitable enterprises outsourced to corporations. An array of capitalist groups develops an interest in generating and sustaining social conflict and in expanding systems of warfare, repression, surveillance, and control. Endless low- and high-intensity warfare, simmering conflicts, civil strife, policing, and so on – have helped keep the global economy afloat. This requires conjuring up one enemy and contrived threat after another, from "drugs" to "terrorism," and more recently to the U.S.-instigated New Cold War. As the post-WWII international order crumbles, the game is changing. The Russian invasion of Ukraine and the U.S.-NATO response have paved the way for a more sweeping militarization of the global economy and society. It has legitimated an expansion of military and security budgets as well as surveillance and repression around the world, not just in North America and the NATO countries.

LINKS: Following the fall of the Soviet Union and the end of the Cold War, global politics seemed dominated by wars that sought to reinforce U.S. imperialism's role as the sole global hegemon. However, in more recent years, a shift appears to be taking place. As the United States has been forced to withdraw from Afghanistan, we have seen Russia invade Ukraine and nations such as Turkey and Saudi Arabia flexing their military power beyond their borders. In general terms, how would you understand the current dynamics at play within global capitalism? How does this fit in with your ideas of a global police state and militarized accumulation?

WIR: The global political and economic are severely out of synch. We have a globally integrated economy that operates within a post-WWII international order that is anachronistic and utterly incapable of stabilizing the system. The political and economic architecture of the post-World War II international order was already crumbling prior to the Russian invasion of Ukraine. That invasion and the West's radical political, military, and economic response to it was but its *coup de grâce*. The United States is no longer the market of last resort and nor can it continue to serve as the liquidity provider of last resort. The political control afforded to the U.S. state by a dollar-denominated global economy is at odds with increasing political multipolarity and with global trade and economic integration. Trading in alternative currencies is a sign of the transformations underway. Yet as U.S. hegemony unravels no new nation-state, at least at this time, can provide the authority structure to stabilize the now inextricably integrated global economy.

Meanwhile, we have to acknowledge that the reason why Chinese-based capitalists or capitalists from other countries that are now exporting their capital around the world can invest in Latin America, Africa, and elsewhere, without first sending in their own military forces or organizing coup d'états, is because five centuries of colonialism and imperialism have already opened up the world to transnational capital and, until recently, the U.S. imperialist machine has kept it open. To take one example, Vietnam was bombed back into the stone age by the United States, left utterly destroyed and in ruins by French and U.S. imperialists, and then subject to devastating sanctions. The country then had no choice but to then open but to transnational capital and integrate into the new circuits of global accumulation. Today Chinese-based, Western-Based, Indian-based, Saudi-based, and Mexican, and Brazilian-based capitalists, along with Vietnamese capitalists themselves, can trade and invest in Vietnam and exploit Vietnamese labor thanks to that imperialism. The traditional Western core already did the dirty work. This may be a very tough analysis for some on the left to swallow but that does not make it less true.

LINKS: Global politics today seems dominated by the growing conflict between the U.S. and China, one that would seem to indicate the end of globalization and a turn toward protectionism, rival trading blocs, and potential war. To this we could add the specter of 21st century fascism, which you have also written about. How can we best understand this growing rivalry and rise of 21st century fascism? How do you view the role of China, Russia, and

BRICS within global capitalism today and the concept of multipolarity promoted by sections of the left?

WIR: If by globalization we are referring to the rise of truly transnational capital and the integration of every country into a globalized system of production, finance, and services, we are surely not seeing an end to capitalist globalization but rather its intensification along with its geopolitical reconfiguration. In fact, trade in intermediate goods constitutes over half of all global trade and according to the UN's trade and development organization UNCTAD, worldwide trade actually reached an all-time high in 2021.

No national or regional economy can survive outside of its integration into the larger global economy. As I already discussed, the national bourgeoises of the larger countries, and even many smaller ones, in the former Third World have been in a process of rapid transnationalization. There is a massive new wave of capital exports out of these countries, including ones we have already mentioned, China, Saudi Arabia, Turkey, and so on.

Even if it wanted to, the TCC is too dependent on an open and integrated global economy for the continued accumulation of capital and power on a world scale to withdraw back into the confines of national economies. The corporate managers of the global economy are entangled in geographic restructuring in accordance with how the political winds are shaping the opportunities for and constraints on accumulation around the world. Transnational capitalists (including Chinese transnational capitalists) are relocating from China to Vietnam, for instance, because of Chinese state constraints on their freedom, U.S. state pressure, or most often simply for cheaper labor, while some Chinese-based transnational capitalists are investing in the so-called industrial renaissance in the United States directly, or indirectly by investing in Mexico, in order to get inside tariff walls and political restrictions.

We need therefore to focus on the contradiction between a globally integrated economy and a nation-state-based system of political domination and capitalist reproduction. This contradiction is becoming ever more acute. It contributes to the escalation of international tensions and throws states around the world into spiraling crises of legitimacy. Transnational capital has only one objective, endless accumulation. But states must deal with the fallout of global capitalism's crisis. They must achieve legitimacy and reproduce the national social formation of the countries over which they rule, keep the domestic order from fracturing, sustain growth, maintain stability and social control, and compete with other states to attract transnationally mobile capital. States must keep positive trade balances whereas transnational capital could care less so long as it is able to freely trade and invest. Unlike global capitalists, state and political elites reproduce their status within the nation-state and its relation to other states and the international system. In the more powerful national states these elites seek aggrandizement. Theoretically speaking, states and state elites, in order to reproduce themselves, must reproduce capital. While states come under pressure from capital to serve its accumulation imperative they also come under pressure from working and popular classes, especially as class struggle and political conflict heat up as we are now seeing.

Not every national state has the same capacities to juggle such destabilizing contradictions while reproducing capital. Stronger ones attempt to sublimate and externalize social and political tensions to other countries and regions. The Chinese state, intent on keeping a lid on rising discontent, announced recently that its goal was to reduce inequality. But the Chinese state must also reproduce capital inside China. The contradictory mandates of states may place them in conflict with one another and with transnational capital. As global capitalist crisis intensifies it pushes states toward nationalism, populism, and protectionism, whether this refers to U.S. protectionism or the Chinese state's crackdown on tech billionaires.

Moreover, there are local, national and regional capitalist fractions that do not have the same capacity as transnational capitalists and compete over local policies and regional control. The temptation here, however, is to make some inappropriate distinction between "national capital" and "imperialist capital," which is an utter analytical and ideological confusion. Capital has only one intention and that is to exploit labor so as to accumulate. Some capitals are able to do so across multiple borders and in the global system at large while others are more limited in their scope yet they enter global circuits through the financial system and other mechanisms of integration. It is a matter of empirical investigation as to whether more local and nationally-grounded fractions of capital are able to influence states in their interests or in their competition with transnational capital.

The impulse toward nationalism, populism, and protectionism comes from states facing the destabilizing conditions of capitalist globalization and crisis yet there is no evidence that the TCC has supported this protectionism. The principal capitalist conglomerates based in the United States and China have experienced an ongoing process of cross-penetration and integration in recent decades that far from reversing has actually deepened even in the midst of the New Cold War. The U.S. and the Chinese states have been taking measures to undercut this integration against the wishes to the TCC. It should come as no surprise that the U.S. Chamber of Commerce has opposed U.S. tariffs and other restrictions of the free movement of transnational capital. The TCC wants access to the whole world without state interference.

Protectionism is a policy of states to attract transnational investment and to appease domestic political unrest. Transnational capitalists will invest wherever they find the best conditions to make profit. State subsidies are on the rise around the world to attract transnational capital in search of investment opportunities. Both the Trump and the Biden governments have pursued subsidies, tax credits and tariffs to entice transnational investors, triggering subsidy and protectionist wars with the EU and China. The Biden administration has restricted investments in Chinese entities involved in semiconductors, microelectronics, and artificial intelligence systems. But the giant tech transnationals do not support these policies. Elon Musk, Tim Cook, and Bill Gates have been among a flood of high-profile business executives who have visiting China in recent months to discuss their expanded presence in China.

We are moving into a multipolar or polycentric world polity within a single integrated global economy exhibiting several centers of intense transnational accumulation such as the North American free-trade bloc, the EU, and a Sino-centric Asian economic region. As I noted in an essay I published on these matters in summer 2023, "The Unbearable Manicheanism of the 'Anti-Imperialist' Left," the emerging global capitalist pluralism may offer greater maneuvering room for popular struggles around the world but a politically multipolar world does not mean that emerging poles of global capitalism are any less exploitative or oppressive than the established centers. Naturally I am simplifying things. There are many levels of mediation and political considerations beyond the broad generalizations I put forward here.

LINKS: Do you see any possibilities for building bridges between anti-imperialist struggles internationally, taking into consideration that local movements might seek support (and even military aid, such as in the case of Ukraine) from different imperialist countries? Can the left advance a position of non-alignment with blocs (neutrality) without abandoning solidarity? What should a 21st internationalism that is both anti-imperialist and anti-fascist look like?

WIR: We face an empire of global capital. I do not think that anti-imperialist struggles can be separated from anti-capitalist struggles. Speaking in generalities, the U.S. state as an institution remains the greatest threat to the world's people. However, it is beyond me why any socialist would think that in order to oppose U.S. interventionism we must turn a blind eye to capitalist exploitation and oppression in other countries around the world or fail to support those resisting such exploitation and oppression. Why should the left advocate for supporting one or another capitalist country or bloc in place of a revitalized proletarian internationalism based on supporting working and popular class struggles in each country and bloc?

Nationalism is intended to obscure transnational class interests and fuels the competition among working classes of different countries. It is, as Rosa Luxemburg noted long ago, an instrument to betray the working class, a tool of counterrevolutionary class politics. We see hyper-nationalism on the rise around the world – in the United States, China, Russia, India, and Turkey, for instance, often with an ethnic component, precisely at a time when global capitalism faces a severe crisis and mass discontent is rising. Socialists have to combat this nationalism. Fascism is always founded on militaristic and chauvinistic nationalism and in response to capitalist crisis. We are in a tragic situation around the world in which a popular revulsion with the global capitalist status quo and mass rebellion from below is breaking out everywhere at a time when the organized socialist left is weak or even nonexistent in many countries. The lack of a clear socialist message and project opens space for authoritarian populists, fascists, and warmongers to manipulate the legitimate grievances among popular sectors facing despair.

We are at an urgent historical juncture. Global capitalism is in a structural crisis of overaccumulation, and political crisis of state legitimacy, capitalist hegemony and international conflict, and an environmental crisis of the planetary ecosystem. Our survival hangs on a thread. The biggest immediate danger we face, apart from the collapse of the biosphere, is fascism and World War III. The breakdown of hegemonic order in earlier epochs of world capitalism were marked by political instability, intense class and social struggles, wars, and ruptures in the established international system. This time, however, the stakes are higher.

Palestine and global crisis: Why genocide? Why now?

William I. Robinson, January 2024

"Genocides are never declared in advance," warned Adila Hassim of the South African legal team. This was in her opening statements before the International Court of Justice (ICJ), convened in January 2024 to hear the charge against Israel for the Crime of Genocide, which is defined by the United Nations Convention as a crime committed with the intent to destroy a national, ethnic, racial, or religious group, in whole or in part.

But this is not necessarily true in the case of Palestine. The destruction of the Palestinian people is perhaps as close as the world can get to a genocide foretold. The signs that the Jewish state was moving toward genocide have been multiplying for years. The possibility has been inherent to the Zionist project, which, from its inception in the late nineteenth century, set as its goal the establishment of a Jewish-only state in the land of Palestine.

The initial months of siege on Gaza appeared to crystallize a Washington–NATO–Tel Aviv axis prepared to normalize genocide even at great political cost. Yet the Palestinian plight has touched a raw nerve among mass publics around the world, especially among youth, giving new energy to the global revolt of the working and popular classes that has been gaining momentum in recent years and heightening the political contradictions of the crisis. There has been an extraordinary outpouring of solidarity with Palestine, including among a younger generation of Jews who do not identify with Zionism and the Jewish state. The Palestinian flag, raised around the world in street demonstrations, at sporting events, and on social media platforms, has become a symbol of popular rage and global intifada against the prevailing status quo.

Genocide could never be carried out without the backing, implicit or explicit, of the ruling groups from the Western heartland of transnational capitalism that under U.S. leadership have served as Israel's principal sponsors. Diplomatic protestations notwithstanding, what may have now made genocide acceptable to these ruling groups is the escalating crisis of global capitalism. The system faces a structural crisis of overaccumulation and chronic stagnation. But the ruling groups also face a political crisis of state legitimacy, capitalist hegemony, and widespread social disintegration; an international crisis of geopolitical confrontation; and an ecological crisis of epochal proportions. Israel's campaign in Gaza constitutes a horrific experiment in how the ruling groups may mold interminable political chaos and financial instability into a new and more deadly phase of global capitalism aimed at violently cracking open new spaces for capitalist expansion and imposing more coercive political methods of social control, from authoritarianism and dictatorship to outright fascism, in an attempt to contain popular rebellion and the rapidly expanding ranks of surplus humanity.

Genocidal pressures were building up against the Palestinians well before the siege of Gaza that began in the wake of the October 7, 2023 Hamas attack. In Israel it is now perfectly normal to call for genocide against the Palestinians, whereas, to the contrary, it is looked upon as treason to defend Palestinian life. Calls were already growing in Israel for ethnic cleansing and genocide against Gazans in the days leading up to the previous largescale assault on the territory in 2014, Operation Protective Edge. Typical of the public discourse in the media, the government, and civil society during that assault was a *Times of Israel* op-ed titled "When Genocide is Permissible." The editorial claimed that "there's going to have to come a time where Israel feels threatened enough where it has no other choice but to defy international warnings." It went on: "What other way then is there to deal with an enemy of this nature other than obliterate them completely? Prime Minister Benjamin Netanyahu clearly stated at the outset of this incursion [Protective Edge] that his objective is to restore a sustainable quiet for the citizens of Israel ... If political leaders and military experts determine that the only way to achieve its goal of sustaining quiet is through genocide is it then permissible to achieve those responsible goals?"

Echoing these sentiments, the Deputy Speaker of the Israeli parliament at the time and a member of Prime Minister Benjamin Netanyahu's Likud party, Moshe Feiglin, urged the Israeli army to kill Palestinians in Gaza indiscriminately and use every means possible to get them to leave. "Sinai is not far from Gaza and they can leave.

this will be the limit of Israel's humanitarian efforts," he said. "The IDF [Israeli Defense Forces] will conquer the entire Gaza, using all the means necessary to minimize any harm to our soldiers, with no other considerations. ... The enemy population that is innocent of wrong-doing and separated itself from the armed terrorists will be treated in accordance with international law and will be allowed to leave."

Some of the right-wing protesters who beat leftists demonstrating in Tel Aviv during Operation Protective Edge wore T-shirts bearing neo-Nazi symbols and photos, including T-shirts bearing the slogan "Good night left side," a neo-Nazi slogan popular in Europe at rock concerts by far-right bands, as a response to the original anti-fascist slogan: "Good night white pride." Nearly one-half of the Jewish population of Israel at the time stated that they supported a policy of ethnic cleansing of Palestinians, and major portions of the population supported complete annexation of the occupied territories and the establishment of an apartheid state.

Between 2014 and 2023, the political climate in Israel continued to shift so sharply to the right that a fascist discourse became palpable in the daily life of the country, with government officials calling for new rounds of ethnic cleansing to expand Jewish settlements in the West Bank and promoting an escalation of settler violence and IDF attacks. In the wake of the October 7 Hamas attack, the Zionist project, founded on systematic ethnic cleansing and terrorism against the Palestinians, went from slow-motion to a full-on, real-time campaign of genocide against Gazans. The South Africa brief presented to the ICJ documented the torrent of statements by government officials at the highest levels of the Jewish state showing clear intent to commit genocide. What are the underlying structural roots in the Israeli and global political economy that are bringing about genocide? And what does the Israeli genocide tell us more generally about the crisis of global capitalism and what the future may hold?

The Palestinian proletariat and the globalization of Israel

Israel's rapid globalization, starting in the late 1980s, coincided with the two Palestinian *intifadas* (uprisings) and with the Oslo Accords, which were negotiated from 1991 to 1993 and then broke down in the following years. Backed by and nudged on by the U.S. and transnational elites as the Cold War wound down, as well as by powerful Israeli capitalist groups, Israeli rulers entered into negotiations with the Palestinian leadership in the 1990s in large part as a response to the escalation of Palestinian resistance in the form of the first intifada (1987–1991). The Oslo Accords, signed in 1993, turned over a Bantustan-like autonomy to the Palestinian Authority (PA) in the occupied territories for what was supposed to be a five-year interim period leading to a final settlement that would end the occupation and establish a sovereign Palestinian state. Yet during the Oslo period from 1991 to 2003, when the process finally broke down altogether, the Israeli occupation of the West Bank and Gaza greatly intensified. Why did this "peace process" break down?

First, the process was not intended to resolve the plight of the dispossessed Palestinian majority. It aimed to integrate an emergent Palestinian elite into the new global order by giving them a stake in defending that order. The PA was expected to mediate transnational capital accumulation in the occupied territories while internally policing the Palestinian masses. In exchange, the "peace process" allowed the Palestinian bourgeoisie to engage in a state-building process, no matter how truncated and emasculated that state. It has been shown in fact that Palestinian class formation during this time involved the rise of transnationally oriented Palestinian capitalists integrated with Gulf capital elsewhere and hoping to convert a new Palestinian state into a platform for its own class consolidation.

Second, the Israeli economy globalized based on a high-tech military–security–surveillance complex. There has been an ever-deeper interpenetration of Israeli capital with transnational corporate capital from North America, Europe, Asia, and elsewhere. Oslo helped this process along, facilitating an Israeli transnational capitalist presence throughout the Middle East and beyond, in part by allowing conservative Arab regimes to lift the regional economic boycott of Israel, and in part by negotiating the creation of a Middle East Free Trade Area (MEFTA) that inserted the Israeli economy into regional economic networks and integrated the whole region much more deeply into global capitalism.

And third, closely related, if the Palestinian bourgeoisie has seen its class formation frustrated by Israeli occupation and by its lack of access to a viable state apparatus – helping to explain its increasing collaborationist stance – the Palestinian proletariat has fast been become surplus humanity standing in the way of transnational capital in Israel and the Middle East. Up until the 1990s, The Palestinian proletariat of the occupied territories constituted a cheap labor force and a captive market for Israel and the Palestinian bourgeoisie. But starting in the 1990s and accelerating in recent years, the Israeli economy began to draw on transnational migrant labor from Africa, Asia, and elsewhere, as neoliberalism and crisis have displaced millions in former Third World regions.

The rise of new systems of transnational labor mobility and recruitment have made it possible for dominant groups around the world to reorganize labor markets and recruit transient labor forces that are disenfranchised and easy to control. Transnational migrant workers in Israel need not be subjected to the apartheid system imposed on Palestinians, because their temporary migrant status achieves their social control and disenfranchisement more effectively, and of course because they are not demanding the return of occupied lands and do not have a political claim to a state. While this is a worldwide phenomenon, it has become a particularly attractive option for Israel because it does away with the need for politically troublesome Palestinian labor.

The 1948 Nakba that established the Jewish state involved the violent expulsion of the Palestinians and the expropriation of their land, but also the subordinate incorporation of hundreds of thousands of Palestinian laborers to work on Israeli farms and construction sites, and in industries, caregiving, and other service jobs. It also entailed the conversion of the West Bank into a captive market for Israeli capitalists. Up until globalization took off in the late twentieth century, the relationship of Israel to the Palestinians reflected classical colonialism, in which the colonial power had usurped the land and resources of the colonized and then exploited their labor. But Middle Eastern integration into the global economy and society on the basis of neoliberal economic restructuring, including the well-known litany of measures such as privatization, trade liberalization, IMF-supervised austerity, and World Bank loans, helped spark the spread of mass worker and social movements and grassroots democratization pressures. These were reflected in the Palestinian intifadas, the labor movement across North Africa, mounting social unrest, and most visibly in the 2011 Arab Spring uprisings.

This tidal wave of resistance, starting with the first intifada, aggravated the historic tension between the drive to ethnically cleanse the Jewish state and the need it had for cheap, ethnically demarcated labor. Starting in the 1990s, Israel began to resolve this tension between dispossession / super-exploitation and dispossession / expulsion in favor of the latter. By the 2000s, hundreds of thousands of migrant workers – by some estimates up to six hundred thousand – from Thailand, China, Nepal, Sri Lanka, India, Eastern Europe, the Philippines, Kenya, and elsewhere came to form the predominant labor force in Israeli agribusiness under the same precarious conditions of super-exploitation and discrimination that migrant workers face around the world. In the wake of the October 7 Hamas attack, Israel deported thousands of Palestinian workers back to Gaza, while Israeli companies asked the government to allow them to hire a hundred thousand Indian workers to replace them. By early 2024, even in the midst of war, thousands of Indian workers were pouring into Israel.

As immigration has reduced Israel's need for cheap Palestinian labor, the Palestinians have become an ever more marginalized surplus population. It is no wonder, then, that in 1993 – precisely the year the Oslo Accords were signed and went into effect – Israel imposed its new policy, known as "closure" – that is, sealing off Palestinians into the occupied territories, ethnic cleansing, and a sharp escalation of settler colonialism. In 1993, the year the "closure" policy began, per capita GNP in the occupied territories plummeted by 30 per cent. By 2007, the rates of unemployment and poverty had topped 70 per cent. From 1993 to 2000 – supposedly the years in which a "peace" agreement was being implemented that called for an end to the Israeli occupation – Israeli settlers in the West Bank doubled to four hundred thousand, then climbed to half a million by the mid-2010s, and reached seven hundred thousand by 2023. Well before the Israeli genocide started in October 2023, acute malnutrition in Gaza was on the same scale as in some of the poorest nations in the world, with more than half of Palestinian families eating only one meal a day.

Among the distinct types of racist structures observed in the sociology of race/ethnic relations, two stand out with regard to

Palestine. One is super-exploitation / disorganization of the working class. This is a situation in which the subordinate and oppressed sector within the exploited classes occupies the lowest rungs of the particular economy and society within a racially or ethnically stratified working class. Key here is that the labor of the subordinate group – that is, their bodies, their existence – is needed by the dominant system, even if the group experiences cultural and social marginalization and political disenfranchisement. This was the historical post-slavery experience of African Americans and Chicanos in the United States, as well as that of the Irish in Britain, Mayan Indians in Guatemala, Africans in South Africa under apartheid, and ethnically demarcated migrant labor, largely Mexican and Central American, presently in the United States.

The other essential racist structure is exclusion and appropriation of natural resources. This is a situation in which dominant groups need the resources of the subordinate group but not their labor – that is, *not* their bodies, their physical existence. This is the racist structure most likely to lead to genocide. It was the experience of the indigenous Indians in North America: dominant groups needed their land but not their labor or their bodies – since African slaves and European immigrants provided the labor needed for the new system – and so they experienced genocide. Now, like the Native Americans before them – and unlike the black South Africans – Palestinian bodies are no longer needed and simply stand in the way of the Zionist state, the settlers and would-be settlers, and transnational capital who need Palestinian land and the wealth that lies beneath it. This shift to surplus humanity is most advanced for Gazans, who have been relegated to the concentration camp that Gaza has been since 2007, when Israel locked them into the strip and imposed a total blockade.

It should come as no surprise, given this context, that the noted Israeli historian Benny Morris, a professor at Ben Gurion University of the Negev who closely identifies with Israel, gave a lengthy interview to the Israeli newspaper *Haaretz* in 2004 in which he referred to the genocide of Native Americans in what is today the United States in order to suggest that genocide may be acceptable. He said in the interview "even the great American democracy could not have been created without the annihilation of the Indians. There are cases in which the overall, final good justifies harsh and cruel acts that are committed in the course of history." He then went on to call for ethnic cleansing of the Palestinians, saying "something like a cage has to be built for them. I know it sounds terrible. It is really cruel. But there is no choice. There is a wild animal there that has to be locked up in one way or another." When I first quoted Morris in an article on Operation Protective Edge in 2014, I stated that his views did not represent consensus inside Israel, but this may no longer be true. Two months into the current genocide, over 80 per cent of Israelis supported the ethnic cleansing of Gaza.

The political economy of twenty-first century genocide

If the problem of surplus capital is endemic to capitalism, over the past couple of decades it has reached extraordinary levels. As global markets become saturated, the leading transnational corporations and financial conglomerates have registered record profits at the same time that income has dropped for a majority, and corporate investment has declined. In the first 18 months after the Covid pandemic, from 2022 to mid-2023, the 148 largest corporate conglomerates in the world increased their total net profits by $1.8 trillion, a 52 per cent jump, while workers lost a combined $1.5 trillion in income. The transnational capitalist class (TCC) has accumulated more wealth than it can possibly spend, much less reinvest. The more the TCC accumulates, the more desperate searches it must undertake for new outlets to unload this expanding mass of profits. Financial speculation, debt-driven growth, and the plunder of public finance are reaching their limits as temporary fixes in the face of chronic stagnation. New outlets to unload surplus accumulated capital must be violently cracked open.

Surplus capital finds its alter ego in surplus labor, as crises of overaccumulation expand the two antagonistic poles of this dialectical unity. The process of capitalist development "constantly produces and produces in direct ratio of its own energy and extent, a relatively redundant population of laborers, i.e., a population of greater extent that suffices for the average needs of the self-expansion of capital, and therefore a surplus-population," noted Marx in *Capital*. "*This is the absolute general law of capitalist accumulation.*" Decades of globalization and neoliberalism have relegated great masses of people around the world to marginal existence. In the coming years, new technologies based on artificial intelligence, combined with displacement generated by conflict, economic collapse, and climate change, will exponentially increase the ranks of surplus humanity. Gaza thus becomes a potent symbol of the plight of the dispossessed around the world, a terrifying mirror reflecting possible futures for masses of people for whom capital has no need.

Yet Israel remains a special case with its own historical specificity of colonialism, apartheid, and fascist foundational ideology. The twentieth century saw at least five cases of acknowledged genocide, and in reality, likely considerably more than five. The Israeli genocide, however, may be most comparable to that of the Nazis, as in the big picture both are responses to a general crisis of world capitalist breakdown. Genocidal pressures have been built into the Zionist project since its birth in the late nineteenth century, insofar as it called for an exclusively Jewish state cleansed of Palestinians. This is why most of us around the world fighting against this genocide condemned the October 7 Hamas attack, but also insisted that this conflict began not in 2023 but in 1948 with the incarnation of that project in the establishment of the Jewish state.

That year, some of the most prominent Jewish individuals worldwide, among them Albert Einstein, Hannah Arendt, Sidney Hook, and Isidore Abramowitz, published a letter to the editor of *The New York Times* warning that "among the most disturbing political phenomena of our times is the emergence in the newly created state of Israel of the 'Freedom Party,' a political party closely akin in its organization, methods, political philosophy and social appeal to the Nazi and fascist parties." The letter went on to warn that the members of the party, which later became the now-ruling Likud party, "speak of freedom, democracy and anti-imperialism, whereas until recently they openly preached the doctrine of the Fascist state."

The Zionist "hasbara," or propaganda machinery, has turned such comparisons between Zionism and Nazism into a taboo, yet the comparison is historically and analytically important. Both Zionism and Nazism emerged from the wave of racial nationalism that swept Europe in the late nineteenth century, according to which all people belong to one or another "racially pure" groups that can be traced back to mythical origins and that correspond to racially pure people-nations. Germany was exclusively for the Aryan race going back to Teutonic tribes and earlier, the French going back to Gaul, the British to the Anglo-Saxons, and the Jews to ancient Jewish kingdoms in Palestine. Campaigns of "blood and soil" were to organize the world according to this ideology. Build into the campaigns of blood and soil that sprung from racial nationalism were expulsion, apartheid, and the specter of genocide.

In order to legitimate conquest, ethnic cleansing, and settler colonialism, the Zionist program of blood and soil in Palestine required the invention of a "Jewish people" that belongs to an ancient Jewish homeland – a foundational myth that would convert a faith community among diverse cultures, places, and histories into a racially pure Jewish people-nation that must return to its ancestral homeland. For this to happen, Palestinians had to be removed and erased from history. Zionists and defenders of the Israeli state take great offense at this analogy between the Nazis and Israeli state actions, including the charge of genocide, in part because the Jewish holocaust is used by the Israeli state and the Zionist political project as a mechanism of legitimation, so that to draw such analogies is to undermine Israel's legitimating discourse. It is crucial to point this out, because that discourse legitimates genocide at the present time. Jewish grief and memory of the holocaust must be weaponized. In order for Jews to be swept up into Zionism, they must be made to feel that there is an existential threat from which they can only be protected by blind defense of Israel, even if this means support for genocide of the Palestinians along with the criminalization of Israel's critics.

Israel thus brings home the tension worldwide between the economic need that ruling groups have for super-exploitable labor, and the political need they have to neutralize the actual and potential rebellion of surplus humanity. Ruling-class strategies of containment become paramount, and borders between national jurisdictions become war zones and zones of death. Palestine is one such death zone, the most egregious perhaps, because it is tied to occupation, apartheid, and ethnic cleansing. Yet tens of thousands have died along the U.S.–Mexico border and North Africa–Middle East–Europe corridors, and in other borderlands between surplus humanity and zones of intense accumulation in the global economy. Just two months before the Hamas attack, it was reported that Saudi border guards opened fire without warning and killed in cold blood hundreds of Ethiopian migrants trying to join 750,000 of their countrymen already working in the Kingdom.

The death cult of global capitalism in crisis

The siege of Gaza and the West Bank is a form of primitive accumulation. In late October 2023, as Israeli bombardment intensified, Israel set about granting licenses to transnational energy companies for gas and oil exploration off the Mediterranean coast, part of its plan to become a major regional gas producer and energy hub as well as an alternative to Russian gas for Western Europe. One Israeli real-estate company notorious for building settlements in occupied Palestinian territories published an advertisement in December 2023 for the construction of luxury homes in bombed-out Gaza neighborhoods, while others spoke of resuscitating the Ben Gurion Canal Project that has been dormant since it was originally proposed in the 1960s. The project involves building an alternative to the Egyptian-run Suez Canal that would run from the Gulf of Aqaba across the Negev desert and Gaza, out to the Mediterranean. The only thing stopping the newly-revised canal project is the presence of Palestinians in Gaza.

The Israeli economy is well equipped for genocide. It has undergone several waves of restructuring as it has integrated into global capitalism. The first saw a transition from a traditional agricultural and industrial economy toward one based on computer and information technology and high-tech telecommunications. This was followed in the wake of the events of September 11, 2001 and the rapid militarization of global politics by a further shift toward a global military–security–intelligence–surveillance–counter-terrorism technologies complex. Israel has become globalized specifically through the high-tech militarization of its economy. Like the larger global economy of which it is a part, it had come to feed off local, regional, and global violence, conflict, and inequalities. The captive Palestinian population under occupation serves as an expedient target and testing ground for systems of mass repression that have then been exported around the world to control restive populations and surplus humanity.

This militarized accumulation and accumulation by repression have become central to the entire global economy and society. Each new conflict around the world opens up fresh profit-making possibilities to counteract stagnation. Endless rounds of destruction and reconstruction fuel profit-making not just for the arms industry, but for engineering, construction, and related supply firms, high-tech, energy, and numerous other sectors, all integrated with the transnational financial and investment management conglomerates at the center of the global economy. These are the gales of creative destruction, to be followed by booms of reconstruction. There is a convergence between the political need to contain surplus humanity and the economic need to open new spaces for accumulation. Peace may not pay, but in the context of a transnational capitalism in crisis, genocide becomes profitable and politically expedient to the ruling groups. Gaza is a real-time alarm bell that, in the decades to come, genocide may become a political tool for resolving capital's intractable contradiction between surplus capital and surplus humanity.

It is a mistake, and a very big one at that, to reduce the project of genocide in Palestine to the Israeli and Western states. Individual capitalist states and transnational elites outside of the West may condemn the genocide and withdraw political support for Israel, but they are not – and cannot be – against the imperatives of global capital accumulation that undergird the genocidal impulse. To the contrary, political opposition to genocide simultaneous to the promotion of worldwide capitalist expansion is a contradiction internal to the managers of global capitalism.

The 2003 U.S. invasion and occupation of Iraq, followed by the establishment in 1997 of the Middle Eastern Free Trade Area (and a host of related bilateral and multilateral regional and extra-regional free-trade agreements and structural adjustment programs) unleashed a cascade of transnational corporate and financial investment in finance, energy, high-tech, construction, infrastructure, luxury consumption, tourism, and other services. This investment has brough Gulf capital, including trillions of dollars in sovereign wealth funds, together with capital from all around the world, involving the EU, North and Latin America, and Asia. This process has inextricably enmeshed them all in global circuits of accumulation. China has become the region's principal trading partner and an important investor in Israel, including in high-tech military and security. The Middle East–Asia corridor is now a major conduit for global capital. Israeli, Arab, and extra-regional transnational capitalists share common class interests that trump political differences over Palestine, beyond the immediate conjuncture of the Gaza war.

Palestine has become an exemplary space for carrying out extermination on a wider global scale: a site for the exercise of new forms of absolute despotic power that have no need for political legitimacy. This is more than old-fashioned settler colonialism; it is the face of a global capitalist system that can only reproduce through bloodshed, dehumanization, sadism, and annihilation. The fate of the global working and popular classes, including those swept up into and also those thrust out of the global circuits of accumulation, may depend on the outcome of the Israeli genocide. The center is collapsing. The utter bankruptcy of bourgeois liberalism has opened space for populist fascists to manipulate mass insecurity and anxiety over the future. The battle lines being drawn in the Middle East reflect global battle lines. Netanyahu, Trump, Milei, Bolsonaro, Modi – these neofascists represent not aberrations but emerging political forms of the despotic rule of capital.

Notes and sources

Readers can consult the original publications for notes and links.

Globalization: Nine theses on our epoch. First published in *Race and Class*, 1996. https://journals.sagepub.com/doi/abs/10.1177/030639689603800202

Global capitalism, migration labor, and the struggle for justice.
First published in *Class, Race and Corporate Power*, 2014.
https://www.jstor.org/stable/48645524

Global capitalism and the restructuring of education. First published in *Social Justice*, 2017. https://www.jstor.org/stable/26405720

Capital has an International and it is going fascist.
First published in *Globalizations*, 2019.
https://jwsr.pitt.edu/ojs/index.php/jwsr/article/view/954

Passive revolution and the movement against mass incarceration.
First published in *Social Justice*, 2020, 46(4)121-129.
https://www.jstor.org/stable/26952591

Global capitalism post-pandemic. First published in *Race and Class*, 2020.
https://journals.sagepub.com/doi/abs/10.1177/0306396820951999

The travesty of "anti-imperialism".
First published in *Journal of World-Systems Research*, 2023.
https://jwsr.pitt.edu/ojs/jwsr/article/view/1221/1628

Capitalist globalization, transnational class exploitation and the global police state.
First published in *LINKS, International Journal of Socialist Renewal*, 2023.
https://links.org.au/capitalist-globalisation-transnational-class-exploitation-and-global-policestate-interview-william

Palestine and global crisis: Why genocide? Why now?
First published in this volume. Sources for most of the data can be found in the following articles:
https://thephilosophicalsalon.com/gaza-a-ghastly-window-into-the-crisis-of-global-capitalism/
https://truthout.org/articles/israel-has-formed-a-task-force-to-carry-out-covert-campaigns-at-us-universities/

Abbreviations

AI	artificial intelligence
BRICS	Brazil, Russia, India, China, South Africa
CCA	Corrections Corporation of America
CCP	Chinese Communist Party
CIT	computer and information technology
DRC	Democratic Republic of Congo
FDI	foreign direct investment
ICJ	International Court of Justice
IDF	Israeli Defense Forces
ILO	International Labor Organization
IMF	International Monetary Fund
IoT	internet of things
IP	internet protocol
MEFTA	Middle East Free Trade Area
OECD	Organization of Economic Cooperation and Development
OPEC	Organization of Petroleum Exporting Countries
PA	Palestinian Authority
PLA	People's Liberation Army
SACP	South African Communist Party
SSA	social structure of accumulation
TCC	transnational capitalist class
TISA	Trade in Services Agreement
TNC	transnational corporation
TNS	transnational state
UHNWI	ultra-high net worth individuals
UNDP	United Nations Development Program
WSF	World Social Forum
WTO	World Trade Organization

About the publisher

RESISTANCE BOOKS is a radical publisher of internationalist, ecosocialist, and feminist books. Resistance Books publishes books in collaboration with the International Institute for Research and Education (iire.org), and the Fourth International (https://fourth.international). For further information, including a full list of titles available and how to order them, go to the Resistance Books website.

info@resistancebooks.org | www.resistancebooks.org

www.ingramcontent.com/pod-product-compliance
Lightning Source LLC
Chambersburg PA
CBHW071714020426
42333CB00017B/2262